Hey, Holy Spirit, It's Me Again

A Dialogue With the Holy Spirit
on Lessons 1-90 of
A Course in Miracles

Hey, Holy Spirit, It's Me Again

A Dialogue With the Holy Spirit on Lessons 1-90 of A Course in Miracles

Reverend Myron Jones

BOOKS

Winchester, UK
Washington, USA

First published by O-Books, 2012
O-Books is an imprint of John Hunt Publishing Ltd., Laurel House, Station Approach,
Alresford, Hants, SO24 9JH, UK
office1@jhpbooks.net
www.johnhuntpublishing.com

For distributor details and how to order please visit the 'Ordering' section on our website.

ISBN: 978 1 84694 470 3

A CIP catalogue record for this book is available from the British Library.

Design: Stuart Davies

Printed and bound by CPI Group (UK) Ltd, Croydon, CR0 4YY

CONTENTS

Introduction

The one thing I have learned for certain doing the lessons in the Workbook of *A Course in Miracles* is that the Course means exactly what it says. Somehow I managed to avoid that simple truth for most of the years I have studied it. It is not complicated or hard to understand. It is simple. When it doesn't appear simple, it is because I am resisting its simple message. My Creator created me like Himself and nothing has changed. Anything I see or experience or think I am that is not Pure Love is an illusion, a hallucination.

The Course is helping me to reach this realization one gentle step at a time. I have terrified myself with stories of separation from my God for so long that I am easily frightened, and fearful students are poor learners. So the Holy Spirit, the Voice for God, which resides forever in my mind, speaks to my Heart every morning as I look at my Daily Lessons. And every day I become ever more willing to believe His gentle message: that God loves me and holds no grievance against me, and that I remain forever as I was created.

The Workbook for *A Course in Miracles* begins with lessons to help me undo my false beliefs. It starts by helping me to see that I am completely wrong about absolutely everything I think I know. "Nothing I see means anything. I have given everything I see all the meaning it has for me. I do not understand anything I see." What?! How am I supposed to feel about this? At first I didn't believe it, but Jesus does not ask me to believe the lessons, only to do them.

Even that simple instruction to just do them, which asks so little of me, was more than I was willing to do for a very long time. It took me many years to reach the point of surrender that allowed me to complete the Workbook Lessons. At the time I was avoiding the task, I did not think of it that way. I believed the ego voice that said I was too lazy, it was too hard, I didn't understand it, I didn't deserve it. But in retrospect I understand that the part of the mind that does not want to relinquish its story of individuality was scrambling for ways to keep me, Myron, away from this work. In a sense, the ego mind was fighting for its very life.

I had been studying and practicing what I read in the Course for around fifteen years when I finally got on board with the rest of the world and bought my first computer. Up until that point I had mostly studied in isolation. I was thrilled to discover that there was now a wealth of information on the Course available through the Internet. It also made it possible for me to be in contact with other students of the Course.

One of the first places I visited was Pathways of Light (www.pathwaysoflight.org), and on that site I discovered a small group of people studying the Workbook together. The moderator would discuss the lesson as she understood it, and would invite each of us to do the same. I jumped in with both feet! I was so excited to have this opportunity to talk to someone else about this remarkable book and to finally move through the lessons. They seemed so much less threatening with others sharing them with me. This was the first time I had ever completed the lessons, and I experienced a significant shift in understanding from doing this.

A few years later I went through the lessons with Kenneth Wapnick through his dialogues in *Journey through the Workbook* which further enriched my study. Then two other ministers, Paul and Deb Phelps, created a journal to use in conjunction with the Daily Lessons called *Illumination Journal,* which is still available at www.miraclesone.org. I bought a copy in 2007 and began doing my lessons with the Holy Spirit. This book is a collection of some of that very personal journaling. It covers the lessons through the second review.

As I did this journaling I was learning to apply the lessons to my daily life. I was also developing an open and honest relationship with the Holy Spirit in my mind. I was getting in touch with my Divinity through speaking to, and more importantly, listening to, the Holy Spirit as He guided me through the lessons.

Always in the past I have been very upset when I failed to live up to my expectations as I did the lessons. The Holy Spirit spoke to my anxiety.

My first message from Holy Spirit:

Don't worry about what you forget to do during the day. Don't be concerned about what you are learning or how it should happen. Do not judge what you do or what you fail to do. Just allow Me to work in you.

Blank Slate

Lesson 1

Nothing I see means anything.

These first lessons are like erasing the chalkboard. I set aside all I think I know. I am a blank slate on which the truth can be written. Every day I am faced with multiple decisions. If I think I know what anything means, I will rely on my thinking mind to make decisions. What is in the thinking mind? Only what I put there, bits and pieces from the past, all of it based on faulty ego thinking. If I make my decisions based on this information, I guarantee the future will be the same as the past. However, if I choose to recognize that I know nothing, I can ask the Holy Spirit for help.

Holy Spirit: The thinking mind insists on meaning and thinks it must be the one who decides on the meaning, and so it feels anxiety at the thought of not knowing the meaning. Notice this anxiety and give it to Me. As you learn to withdraw all of the meaning you have given the world, you will be wonderfully surprised at how beautiful it is.

Lesson 2

I have given everything I see in this room [on this street, from this window, in this place] all the meaning that it has for me.

Holy Spirit brought to mind a person I had judged. As I thought about him, my mind sifted through all the ways I am judging him as wrong. Suddenly my attention returned to the lesson for today and I realized that I had given this person all the meaning he has for me. So all the things I don't like about him or that make me uncomfortable come from me, not from him.

Holy Spirit, thank You for that insight. I recognize that I have written meaning on this person, and I erase that meaning. I wait for You to write Your meaning there. I recognize that this person is symbolic of everything. I am deeply grateful to You as You gently correct my errors.

Lesson 3

I do not understand anything I see in this room [on this street, from this window, in this place].

The day I did this lesson I was in the middle of a move. Katrina had devastated New Orleans, and then less than a month later, Hurricane Rita devastated the other side of the state including Lake Charles. There was damage to the house where I lived; thus the move. This is the message the Holy Spirit gave me that morning.

Holy Spirit: Precious child, you are willing to start over and to see these lessons as if they were brand new. This is helpful and so appreciated. You are not alone; I will be with you each step of the way. See each day as a classroom in which to study that day's lesson. For instance, today you have plans to write and to pack for your upcoming move. As you sit down to write, accept that you don't know what anything means, and open your mind for Me to help you.

You keep putting off packing because you are frozen in indecision about what to bring and what to discard. Again, recognize that you don't know what anything means and this recognition is an invitation for Me to help you. This job feels so overwhelming to you that you feel like crying when you think of it. Feel Me with you. Allow Me to decide for you. It is such good practice for you. If you begin to feel discouraged recognize that you are packing with the ego, and bring your mind back in line with Me. Moving can be joyful, and if it is not, then something has gone wrong. Simply shift your attention from the ego to Me.

Me: I feel so much better. I did not even realize how much I was dreading this job, and it did not occur to me why. I thank You for Your words and for Your help. You feel like a best friend, only one who is always here, always has time for me, and always knows the answer.

The Holy Spirit was teaching me to use everything in my life as a way to awaken from the dream of separation.

The lessons move us back and forth between what we see to what we think and finally help us understand the connection, the correlation between cause (our thoughts) and effect (what we see).

Lesson 4

These thoughts do not mean anything. They are like the things I see in this room [on this street, from this window, in this place].

My thoughts do not mean anything. How could that be? I have placed such a premium on my ability to think that I am stunned by Lesson 4. What could Jesus mean when he says that my thoughts are such a mixture that I cannot even call them good or bad? As I examine the thoughts arising in my mind I notice that they conflict with each other. As I allow the parade to continue, I notice that some of them are just nonsense. I notice that all of them are the past replaying over and over or the future being endlessly planned. It makes me tired to look at them.

I have noticed before that my thoughts are often just meaningless chatter. Could it be that they are always meaningless chatter? I am told that beneath the meaningless chatter are my real thoughts. It is a relief to know that I have real thoughts, and I am encouraged to practice this lesson so that I can get to them.

After all, I am only being asked to notice my thoughts and to realize that they are meaningless. I'm not asked to make them meaningful or even to quit thinking them. This is not a difficult practice. I can do this.

I laugh at myself when I think how I used to really hate doing these first lessons, because I did not understand their true helpfulness. Now I just read their titles, and my heart swells with joy as I realize how they are helping me remember who I am.

Before I can be aware of meaningful thoughts I must fully realize that I am not thinking them right now. This will take consistent and vigilant effort on my part. These simple beginning steps are really essential in this process. If I continue to depend on the ego-thinking mind, I will not really know anything. As I surrender to Holy Spirit and let go of the desire for the personal, separate mind, knowledge will be given. Accepting that my thoughts are meaningless is the first step toward true surrender.

Holy Spirit: You have been doing this for a long time, dear one. Every time you notice a thought that makes you feel bad and then bring that thought to Me for correction, you are doing this lesson. But now I want you to understand that this means all of your thoughts, not just the ones you have judged as bad. All of your thoughts are meaningless. That is the point of this lesson, to help you see this.

You are thinking that this will be very hard and that it will take all of your time today. Don't make this hard. You don't have to catch every little thought. In fact, that is just an ego concept. One thought, used correctly, would be representative of all thoughts. Just keep your mind open to Me. Remind yourself throughout today of your holy purpose. I will bring to your mind thoughts to use as practice. All I need is your willingness.

Lesson 5

I am never upset for the reason I think.

When I first started doing the lessons, some of them, especially these first lessons, were hard simply because I didn't understand what they meant or why they were important. Now I have started to see the bigger picture and so they make more sense to me. An example is when my son was sick and I was worried about him. I was not worried about Toby for the reason I thought.

I thought I was worried about Toby because I loved him. As I applied the lesson, I noticed that I had resistance to seeing past this one thought. I reminded myself that my thoughts are meaningless and that I have real thoughts beneath them. I did not dig for a deeper, truer meaning, but I did give my willingness to be corrected. I asked the Holy Spirit to help me, because my beliefs were causing me to suffer.

As my willingness increased, I saw many layers of beliefs and some of them were not pretty to look at. I was worried about my son because I was not able to fix him, and it made me feel inadequate as a mother. I was worried about my son because the costs were piling up. I was worried about my son because if he died, I would suffer. I saw many, many reasons why I was worried about him, and it was very painful to see how little most of them had to do with love. In fact, it became obvious to me that I didn't even know what real love was.

It is very hard to let go of some thoughts because they support my sense of identity. The thought, "I think I am worried about my son because I love him," was very hard to release. But I could not keep this one and let another go. If I believe that some of my thoughts are meaningful, I am going to be mired in the ego forever, as I try to pick and choose what is real and what isn't. I will never succeed and so I will never wake up. The way out of hell is to accept that I don't know what anything is for, and to simply do the lessons as indicated. This works, and nothing else I have ever tried has worked.

I love that Jesus is telling us that the form of upset doesn't matter, and even though one upset can look very different from another, all forms of upset are really the same. I love that I can use the different forms of upset, as if they really were different, to learn that they are not different. My favorite concept, though, coming from Lesson 5, is that there are no small upsets. They are all equally disturbing to my mind. What does the cause of the upset matter? How can I see it as big or little? Either I have peace or I don't. I can't have a little peace. It is peace or it isn't. Every upset disturbs my peace, and so they are all the same. I am grateful to know this.

I See. Or Do I?

Lesson 6

I am upset because I see something that is not there.

These lessons proceed in a logical sequence. I begin by recognizing that nothing I see means anything, and then I am told that my thoughts don't mean anything. I am introduced to the idea that I don't know what makes me upset, which is perfectly logical when you consider that my thoughts are meaningless, and it is through my thoughts that I am judging everything. Now I take the next logical step, as Jesus is helping me accept that I am upset because I am seeing something that is not there.

I can use whatever is in front of me at the moment to practice this lesson. I have noticed that my life lines up nicely with whatever lesson I am doing, so I know the perfect circumstances will present themselves so that I can see this clearly. More and more as I do the lessons, I understand that this is what everything is for.

I didn't sleep well and woke up tired and frustrated. I simply accepted this mood as what happens when I don't get enough sleep. I have a rule that says I will be tired unless I get a certain amount of sleep. My meaningless thoughts have convinced me that this is true, and so I experience a meaningless situation. I think I am upset because I am tired and I think I am tired because I did not get enough sleep. Today I am willing to see this differently. I am upset because I see something that is not there.

My willingness allows the Holy Spirit to fill my mind with truth instead of meaningless thoughts. I remember that this is a neutral event, and I am giving it all the meaning it has for me. The only thing that actually happened is that I did not get as much sleep as usual. I then decided that I think that this means I will be tired and frustrated.

I remember that if I could feel tired because I did not get enough sleep, then I would be a victim of the world I see. I know this cannot be true. What these thoughts did was to crack open my mind to the possibility that I am seeing something that is not there, and so I can see something else if I so choose. Once I made that choice, the Holy Spirit did the rest, and this changed everything. I no longer felt tired or listless. For the rest of the day I felt perfectly normal.

Lesson 7

I see only the past.

This lesson tells me that I see only the past, and while I could understand this, I was baffled as to what to do with the information. Am I expected to unlearn that bananas are good for the body because they are rich in potassium? As I opened my mind to the Holy Spirit, He helped me to see that He needs only my vigilant attentiveness and my willingness to be wrong about what I currently believe. In this way He can correct my thinking.

A helpful way to look at this is to see the ego-thinking mind as a filing cabinet stuffed with information I have picked up over the years and filed away in the proper category. All of it is based on perception, which is not truth but simply judgment formulated from partial understanding, and as such it is nearly completely useless. And yet, I base every decision in my life on this information.

If I continue to make decisions based on what happened in the past nothing will ever change. I must say that this sounds exactly like an ego strategy for self-continuance. By continually returning to the past to make decisions in the present, I am making the ego my authority. I am now choosing to return that authority to One Who knows. I am learning to question my beliefs, rather than blindly accept the thoughts in my mind. I now routinely question their validity and ask for clarity from the Holy Spirit, rather than from the ego.

This is not always easy for me to do. I have become very enamored with the idea that my thoughts are valid and meaningful, and I have trouble letting this go. As I was trying to hear the Holy Spirit in my mind, I kept returning to the old ego filing cabinet. My mind wanted to believe that it held a vast store of knowledge when really it held a vast store of useless information.

Holy Spirit, how does this apply to my packing for the move?

Holy Spirit: When you look at each object, you are failing to see it as it is. Instead you are ascribing a meaning to it based on an invalid valuing system. It is invalid because it came from the ego, which doesn't know anything. For instance, you look at that blue tea set and you see it as an affirmation that you are liked and respected by the person who gave it to you.

Look at it with Me, and allow Me to show you what it really is. Can you let go of your meaning long enough to do that? Do you think that you truly need that affirmation of affection and respect? Because that is what you are holding on to; not the teapot itself. I assure you that the affection the giver feels for you is not dependent on the teapot being on your shelf. I further assure you that your worth is not dependent on her respect.

Here is something you can do. Stand before each item in question and invite Me to look at it with you. Just be willing to see it differently. Then do with the object what feels good to you.

Lesson 8

My mind is preoccupied with past thoughts.

I'm not sure I ever really understood the significance of this lesson until today. I know that my mind is filled with past thoughts. When I watch my thoughts I notice just how preoccupied I am with the past. I seem to always be thinking either of something that happened in the past or something that could happen in the future.

Lately I have begun to doubt that I spend very much time in the present at all, and reading this lesson today, I realize that I never spend time in the present. Everything I see is an outward projection of my thoughts. My thoughts are based on the past that doesn't exist and so nothing I "see" exists. It's all an illusion. I knew that, but following the logic, I understand it in a way I never have before.

If I am thinking of the past and the past doesn't exist, I am not really thinking. My mind is not full of thoughts; it is full of nothing. Jesus calls my "thoughts" thoughtless ideas, and these thoughtless ideas preoccupy my mind and keep me from recognizing truth.

I know that I want to quiet the chatter in my mind. I long for a peaceful mind. Now I wonder what is there that I have been missing. I wonder what my real thoughts are. If I were not picturing thoughtless ideas, what would I "see" instead? This changes everything.

Holy Spirit: Did you notice that even as you asked Me for insight, your mind continued to preoccupy itself with past thoughts? Do you see how this works now? Ego protects itself from your real thoughts, your God thoughts, by keeping you distracted, that is, preoccupied with nothing thoughts. It took great effort on your part to shift your focus enough to hear Me. I speak to you always; it is you who are sometimes not engaged in our discourse because you are busy hiding our thoughts from your consciousness. Let us now work together to change this.

Me: I am ready to completely surrender to You, Holy Spirit. I am ready to be completely obedient. I want unimpeded communication with You. I want to hear You clearly and with ease. I am ready to be emptied of past thoughts so that I can be aware of my real thoughts.

Lesson 9

I see nothing as it is now.

Jesus just blew me away in Lesson 8 as he explained why I don't actually have thoughts, and why I don't actually see anything. It is easier now to accept that I see nothing as it is now. What makes this lesson really helpful to me is that Jesus tells me that while I may have an intellectual understanding of these lessons, they don't really mean anything to me right now. He tells me that these exercises are concerned with practice, not with understanding.

It is a slippery concept and hard for me to hold on to. I picture my daughter and I realize I never see her as she is now. When I look at Susan I see her as a baby, her little head on my shoulder as I held it steady. I see a tiny little girl walking to the fence with her hand in mine so we could look at the goat. I see her in a little mouse outfit dancing on the stage.

I see her standing proudly in her new outfit waiting for the bus; performing in her first play; throwing away a second-place ribbon because coming in second is not winning. I see a college graduate; a lesbian; a gifted writer; a woman with her heart broken by her partner. Because I see only the past in her and don't know how to stop, I don't see her. In every moment she creates herself anew and I can't know that person because I hold tightly to my thoughts about her. I do not see this face as it is now.

The ego-mind wants to know more, to understand, but I am going to just practice as indicated. I am going to remind myself all day long that I don't see anything as it is now. Holy Spirit, I am willing.

Lesson 10

My thoughts do not mean anything.

Lesson 10 revisits the idea that my mind is really a blank. Like I am likely to forget that! Well, actually, I do forget it for great stretches of time, but I will continue my practice because I really do want to experience my real thoughts. If I continue to believe that my thoughts are meaningful and important, I will be unwilling to release them. I will never know what my real thoughts are.

At first it felt intensely frightening to think of releasing my thoughts. They do not mean anything, but I have identified with them and so I think they define me. If I release them, who am I? Jesus is telling me that I have real thoughts, but that is not my experience. I am being asked to accept this on faith. But I am being given little, simple exercises; I am taking small, gentle steps.

Each of these little steps is teaching me trust and bringing my awareness closer to my real Self. I am getting used to the idea that the thinking mind is the ego, and I am more comfortable now with the idea that I can let go of it. I am learning to trust, and it is acceptance and practice that are teaching me trust. I am aware now of thoughts that did not come from ego, and this motivates me to practice more.

Holy Spirit: Precious one, you have placed great value on your thoughts, and it is hard to give up what you value. So we begin by introducing the idea that your value is misplaced. Here is a parable for you. A wealthy man goes into his treasure room and looks at his gorgeous treasure chest. He runs his hands over the smooth wood, and the shiny metal. He admires the stones of many colors and varying sizes that are encrusted all over the box. He never tires of admiring this box and each time he looks at it, he notices something he had not seen before. He thinks how lucky he is to have so much and thinks, "I am a rich man."

The man is indeed rich, but it is not the smooth wood and shiny metal and colorful stones that are his wealth. In truth they are worth little. Inside the box is his true wealth, but he has never seen it because he cannot take his eyes off the distractions offered on the surface of his chest.

Dear one, you have been gazing adoringly at the worthless, while under that you have real treasure. The ego provides endless distractions to keep your attention on the meaningless, because if you see your real thoughts you will laugh at the foolishness of the ego and it will disappear.

I assure you that your meaningless thoughts are of no value, and are merely covering your true treasure. They are like dark clouds that block your vision and, like clouds, are insubstantial and easily dispersed. Together, you and I will take the simple steps that will brush away the meaningless and reveal your holy thoughts, the thoughts you think with God. This is your true treasure.

Me: It is true that I have felt some reluctance to let go of what I have for what I don't know, and that I have had trouble accepting that my thoughts are meaningless and that I am not really thinking at all. At first it seemed so strange and hard to understand, but now I accept it, though I still hold on to my own thoughts so I know I need much more practice. I am willing to do what You say because I love You and I trust You. Holy Spirit, You have taught me to value the peace of God, and I want more of it. I give You all the willingness I have, and I give you my doubts and uncertainties as well.

I Am Upset Because I Think I See Something God Did Not Create

Lesson 11

My meaningless thoughts are showing me a meaningless world.

We are about to turn the world on its head with this one! I have spent most of my life believing that I react to situations that occur in the world, and now Jesus tells me that I am completely wrong about that. I was planning to walk at the park today, and when I went outside it was raining and muggy. I felt disappointed. Sound familiar?

In the past, I used to think that I was disappointed because it was raining and I couldn't go for my walk. Rather than saying I was upset that it was raining, it would make more sense to say that that I was upset because of my thoughts about rain. Even more to the point, now that I understand that the world is not the cause of my thoughts, but that my thoughts are the cause of the world, it makes even less sense to blame the world.

The import of this lesson begins to dawn on my mind, and my efforts become a very holy endeavor. I approach this day with a sense of awe. I give it my full willingness, as I allow this idea to take root in my mind.

Holy Spirit: Yes indeed, Myron, we are pulling weeds and planting seeds. Notice how your willingness has made this job far easier this time than it was before. The work you have been doing has prepared the soil, making it loose so that pulling out the weeds (the meaningless thoughts) is easier now. The soil is now richer and the seeds we plant will take root and grow more quickly. Watch how your resistance is beginning to fall away.

Lesson 12

I am upset because I see a meaningless world.

I have always thought that I am frightened by what happened in the world, but really, I am frightened by what happens in my mind. The world has no meaning. If I think that a tornado is a frightening phenomenon, it is because my thoughts about tornados are frightening. If I were a storm chaser, I would find them exciting. They are neither frightening nor exciting. I decide on their meaning with my thoughts about them.

Because my thoughts are meaningless, the world I see is meaningless. This is why I am upset. When I become upset about something going on in my world today, I can recognize that this is just a picture of my meaningless thoughts. There is no truth in it. I can ask the Holy Spirit to correct my thinking. As I do this, I reinforce the truth and open my mind to my real thoughts.

Holy Spirit, as I do this lesson I keep thinking about how I had always thought that my feelings, good or bad, were dependent on what was happening in the world around me. There always seemed to be so much supportive evidence of this. I am learning that this is not true, and this is the first step in this process. Please talk to me about this.

Holy Spirit: You are certainly right that you are not a victim of the world you see, and this is the reason you are not the victim. The world isn't being done to you, but by you. Your thoughts show you a world, and if what you see is upsetting, it is because your thoughts are upsetting. Your thoughts are upsetting because they are meaningless. The world is a blank slate upon which you write your thoughts.

When Toby and Caroline [my son and his friend] *went to Istanbul, your thoughts showed you a very frightening situation. You saw them getting kidnapped by terrorists or their plane being hijacked. You saw them far from home where you could not reach them, if they needed you. In other words, the meaning you gave that trip was very frightening.*

They saw the trip differently. They saw it as an exciting adventure filled with new sights and interesting people. They saw themselves doing something different and fun. They gave the trip a different meaning, because their thoughts were different. But the truth is, neither view was real, because thoughts are meaningless. The meaninglessness is what is upsetting.

While all of this was happening, you kept asking for another way to see it. You were given that new way, but at first you could not accept it. It was hard for you to take your eyes from that which frightened you. You could not look on both the false and the true, and so you had to choose. As soon as you were able to look away from the fearful picture your thoughts were painting for you, you were filled with peace. The pictures did not change; they were still on that trip and all the possibilities were still there, but you recognized the meaninglessness of them. You surrendered your own interpretation and accepted Mine.

What is becoming obvious is that I cannot get from the meaningless thought to the meaningful true thought with the thinking mind. What I can do is be willing to get there. The Holy Spirit does the rest. That change in mind that has nothing to do with the ego's efforts is the true Miracle.

Lesson 13

A meaningless world engenders fear.

I've already been told that a meaningless world is upsetting, but now in Lesson 13 that upset has been narrowed down to fear. Why is this? I know that because I am preoccupied with past thoughts, my mind is really a blank. What happens now is that I feel challenged to write something there before God does. I am obviously in denial about this and in denial about the fear and guilt this engenders in me.

I only need to look around at the world I see to know that this is not the world God created. I only need to look at my own thoughts to know that they are not the thoughts I think with God. What I see can only be the result of the meaning I have placed on the world.

The ego is afraid to let God write His meaning, because the ego is afraid it will prove to be its demise, and surely it would, for who would choose the meaningless if they recognized meaning? I want to see the truth, so I am learning to give the Holy Spirit what I think I see and ask Him to show me the truth. I still feel some resistance to this. There are so many ways in which the ego writes its meaningless script, using fear to keep me engaged in it.

An example is this book. Even as I write, the ego is chattering away about how I will look to others. If I do not acknowledge the fear that I will be judged, and the fear that I will not be accepted (and all that means to me), the ego will continue to build stories around that fear. Left unchecked, the ego will show me a world so full of judgment that I will be afraid to continue. I will stop writing or begin to write what feels safe, parroting what others say, rather than writing what I really feel.

As an alternative, I can acknowledge the fear that arises as the ego writes its own script and ask the Holy Spirit to help me see differently. I can surrender to Him the little self I created, the self that I designed to impress others, and allow Him to show me my true grandeur as God's Son. It is very frightening sometimes to think of letting go of my creation. It feels like standing naked before the world and hoping they will not ridicule me.

I am going to notice my own miscreations, and acknowledge that they are meaningless. The fear that I experience at this thought is the fear that I am in competition with God. I will do this, knowing that it is a very important step.

Me: Holy Spirit, could You talk to me about this? Why do I still feel discomfort at the idea of a meaningless world?

Holy Spirit: That is only the ego shuddering in fear as it foresees its own death. Do not be concerned by this twinge of resistance. You are completely and wholly supported as you take this next step. Don't think you have to do or undo anything, and don't allow guilt to enter into this process. When you do your lesson, and when you see ways in which you think you are in competition with God, just notice them. Just say, "Oh, I see that," or "So that is how it works." Your willingness to see differently is your part, and that is all. Guilt and fear are just ego devices to keep you from being willing.

Lesson 14

God did not create a meaningless world.

Lesson 14 takes me more deeply into my fear with the words, "God did not create a meaningless world." At first glimpse this would seem to be a comforting thought, but then I think that if God did not create it, where did it come from? It must have come from my mind. This seems to be saying that I am meaningless.

Now I have entered another level of fear and my thoughts go to defense. If I want to defend against my own annihilation, I must defend myself against God, because if I allow Jesus to direct me through these lessons, I will empty my mind of all I once believed. It is clear this is what is happening as each lesson directs me to let go of all I believe to be true. The slate will be blank and God will write His meaning on it.

That means my meaning will cease to exist. This is why the Course said this is frightening. Either I will have to accept my "death" (the death of self) or I will have to beat God to the punch and re-write my own meaning. Either way is horrifying. The Holy Spirit spoke into my Heart as I sat, dizzy with confusion and uncertainty.

Holy Spirit: Precious child, you have done such a good job daring to look at the depth of the ego error. You know that, while all of what you said is true for the ego-self, you are not that ego. You exist in God. It is your Holy Self that, with your Father, gave meaning to creation. It is only the ego world that is meaningless.

Slough off that meaninglessness, and do it gladly, because what you and your Father created lies beneath what the ego made. It takes great courage to step out of the boat and walk on water, but I promise you that I will be walking beside you to hold you up if you falter. I love you, and I am so happy and proud of what you have done this morning. The angels are singing a chorus of Hallelujah!

Me: I know that I am not the ego, but I am also afraid I am. I have been seeing myself small for such a long time, and seeing my glory is such a new thing for me. I trust you, Holy Spirit, my friend and my partner. I trust You to lift me up if I allow my fear to get the better of me. I will do my best to not allow this practice to sink back into mindless affirmations today. Please be with me and help me to remember my holy purpose all through the day. I love You and I appreciate You.

Lesson 15

My thoughts are images that I have made.

In this lesson Jesus says:

"It is because the thoughts you think you think appear as images, so you do not recognize them as nothing. You think you think them, and so you think you see them. This is how your "seeing" was made. This is the function you have given your body's eyes. It is not seeing. It is image making. It takes the place of seeing, replacing vision with illusions."

Well, this lesson never fails to astonish me. It is telling me that I am so wrong about the world I think I see that it is hard to even grasp the error, such is its magnitude. I look around and see all sorts of stuff. I've been looking at all this stuff since the first lesson which helped me begin the process of accepting that how I see everything is a result of the past. I am finally becoming open to the idea that I only see the past in everything.

I'm coming to accept that everything I see is a product of my thoughts and, since these thoughts are rooted in the past, I am not really looking at anything as it is now. In yesterday's lesson I discovered just what it really means that God did not create a meaningless world, and the world I have been looking at is clearly meaningless, so it doesn't exist. Nothing in form exists and never has. Do you feel the floor under you starting to dissolve? I feel like holding on to something so I don't tumble down the rabbit hole. But wait! There is nothing to hold on to!

Today's lesson helps me understand how all of this happened. First, I have to understand that I think I am thinking, but I am not. These thoughts I am so familiar with are not really my thoughts, but I do have real thoughts that I will become aware of when I release the unreal thoughts.

Okay, so I have an unreal thought about a bottle of water. In the past I have learned things about water. So I think about a bottle of water that reflects all of this past learning, and *voila*, Dasani water appears in the illusion. I think I think bottled water, and so bottled water appears. Now I "look" at the bottled water on the table in front of me, and since it seems to be there, it seems to prove that there really is such a thing as bottled water. This is the function I have given my eyes, to convince me that there is a world outside of my mind. My eyes report to me not what is there, but what I believe is there; what I want to be there.

Kenneth Wapnick used a simple demonstration once that stuck with me. He takes a piece of paper, wads it up, and throws it to the floor. Then he turns his back on it and turning around to face it again he appears surprised to see it. He says, "Who put that paper there?" This is what I think of when I read this lesson. I have a thought, I project the thought into the world, it appears as an object, I turn away just long enough to forget that I put it there with my thought, and then I point to the object and say, "There it is. I see it because it exists." Really, what I should be thinking when I see something is, "Look, I see it because I thought it." Thinking comes first, then thinking takes form. I don't see solid objects; I see thought-forms.

I think I think some nonsense and then project it onto the screen of my imagination, and my equally false thought about eyes and their purpose make it possible for me to "see" what is not there, and so convince me further that the illusion is real. Do you have any idea how hard it is going to be to convince myself that all I see is really only images of my thoughts and that none of it exists, not even the eyes that purportedly see them? Of course you do, and so does Jesus. That is why He gave us such simple easy steps to get us there.

How do I apply this to my life? Well, very gently, as Jesus suggests. In my new, deeper understanding of these lessons, I feel like I have something very slippery in my hands, and if I am not careful, I will lose my grip on it. I don't want to lose this, so I am asking the Holy Spirit to be with me while I do these lessons. I am opening up to Him and allowing Him to deepen my understanding.

Holy Spirit: Yes, Myron, you are gaining a new understanding. Do not be afraid of this. You would not have this awareness unless you were ready to look at it. Don't be afraid of losing it, because it is part of your holy mind and has always been there and always will. Your awareness will slip in as you become more willing to see it, and then retreat back when you become fearful, or change your mind about what you are willing to acknowledge, but it will never go away.

Relax about that. Everything really is in perfect order, and you are moving at exactly the right speed. I am with you, holding you up, gently encouraging and helping. I am not concerned that you are going to fail. I am not judging your retreats. I understand, and I know of your ultimate success, so I know there is nothing to fear. Your success is not far in the future, for there is no future. It is right there.

Me: I feel a sense of excitement and anticipation. I do want gentle, easy little steps, Holy Spirit, but I also want to be there! I give this all to You, because the one thing I know for sure is that I do not want to make any decisions without You. Thank You. I love You.

The Effects of How I See

Lesson 16

I have no neutral thoughts.

Lesson 16 builds on Lesson 15. I have no neutral thoughts. Everything I see with my eyes is created through my thoughts. *There is no exception to this.* If it is a true thought it contributes to what is true, and if it is a false thought it adds to the illusion. I cannot simply dismiss my thoughts as unimportant. In the past I have been tempted to ignore ego-thoughts as untrue, and thus unimportant, but these thoughts have constructed an entire world. It may be an illusory world, but it is an illusion I believe in and so experience.

I had plans this morning, and from the moment I woke up, it was as if the world were conspiring to undo them. I am looking at my thoughts about this. My first thought was, "I'm not going to finish my work." I feel anxious when I think this. I realize that this is not a neutral thought. It is a false thought, because it implies that I am a victim of the world and that I know what this morning is for. It implies that I am vulnerable and powerless. This thought adds to the illusion. I ask the Holy Spirit to correct my thinking.

After I had the thought that I was not going to finish my work and that I needed to get it done, I noticed that I also had the thought that this was not a true thought and that I didn't have to believe it. This is a true thought and adds to the Kingdom. It was this thought that brought me to the Holy Spirit for correction.

The first thought leads directly to war. If I believe that the morning should be different than it is, I go to war with the world that seems to be intruding on my plans. The second thought leads to peace. I don't know what this day is for. I surrender it to the Holy Spirit and trust that it will unfold as it should.

There are no idle thoughts. They all create according to their kind. And as is always true, it is very simple. Each thought is only true or false; each thought creates peace or war. That is all that matters. I don't need to go more deeply than that. My thoughts are creating my world. Are they creating a peaceful world or a world at war? Are they adding to the Kingdom or to the illusion?

Holy Spirit, I know what to do. I have had a lot of practice looking at my thoughts and bringing them to You. Now I intend to take this to a new level with the realization that all thoughts, not just some, are creating my world as I believe them. The ones that cause immediate or unavoidable results are no more important than the ones I hardly notice. I ask for Your support in this because, honestly, it feels like a never-ending job. Also, the idea of success scares the bejeepers out of the ego.

Lesson 17

I see no neutral things.

Yesterday I learned that I have no neutral thoughts. I also learned that all thoughts are creative according to their likeness, either true or false. Today I see this projected into the world, so what I see is not neutral either, but must reflect truth or error.

As I was taking a shower, I thought about this. I was looking at a jar of foot scrub and thought that it was neither more nor less important than anything else, so I used it as part of my lesson. The more I thought about it, the more amazed I was at the meaning I have given this jar of foot scrub. So many thoughts went into putting these bath items in my life. I thought about how happy I was with the color, and that brought to mind the bath crystals that were a disappointment color-wise. I chose their color, then regretted it and felt "wrong" for doing it.

As I looked at the jar I saw that it represented for me the love I was lavishing on myself in buying it, and so I gave the jar of foot scrub the job of making me feel loved. I thought about spending too much money on these kinds of things and wondered if spending my retirement money on foot scrub was going to condemn me to spending my retirement in a box under a bridge with the other homeless folks.

Did I ever think that this was just a jar of foot scrub? Did I think that the thoughts behind this jar were neutral? I thought this was just a simple impulse purchase, so there was a temptation to think of this as neutral, just some foot scrub. Without the meaning I gave it the foot scrub would be neutral, but clearly it was charged with all sorts of meaning that I made up for it.

Lesson 18

I am not alone in experiencing the effects of my seeing.

There are three main points in this lesson.

- All thoughts give rise to what I see. ("All thinking produces form at some level.") Therefore all thoughts are important.
- Minds are joined; therefore, I affect others, and at the same time, I affect the whole.
- The emphasis is on how I see, rather than what I see.

I am, of course, reminded of the line from the Course which tells me I have no idle thoughts. The first time I read that, I realized I was reading something very important, but my mind boggled at the thought and so I did not dwell on it for long. It took many years for me to accept that there was no getting around this. It was then that I chose to become vigilant in watching my thoughts and began to ask for correction.

When I began moving into my house, there seemed to be a hundred little things (and one big one) that needed correction. It began to seem all just too much, and I noticed that I was feeling weepy. So, I began to notice my thoughts. I realized that many of them were blame thoughts. This person should have done that, that contractor did this wrong and now is long gone and I am left to fix it. The list was very long and nearly everybody got some of the blame.

So what I did was to begin the undoing of these ego-thoughts. I noticed that when I blamed someone for not doing their job right, I was really saying that I felt overwhelmed and discouraged and that it was the other person's fault that I felt that way. I changed my mind about that. I took responsibility for my feelings and accepted that these contractors all did what they did, and if I had feelings about it, that was my choice. The contractors didn't make me feel anything.

I had many thoughts yesterday that I know will have far-reaching effects if I simply allow them to go unchecked. For instance, if I blame my brother for how I feel, I teach myself that I am the victim of the world I see. I also teach myself and the other person that we are separate individuals with separate interests, and one of us is going to have those interests satisfied, and one of us is going to lose.

These are not ideas I want to teach because these are not ideas I want to learn. I teach my brother through what I do and say, but I also teach through the thoughts I choose to believe. We are one mind; what I think affects the entire mind. As the lesson says, "It is therefore in my power to change every mind along with mine, for mine is the power of God."

The Holy Spirit communicates to me in many ways. Sometimes when I ask for help, He gives me His thoughts in a way that is useful to me. Sometimes it is less a thought and more as if He were comforting and supporting me, which I then put into words as I understand it. This time it was both. I felt overwhelmed with the circumstances and with my seeming inability to use what I have learned from Him to see this differently.

I was experiencing the moment as chaotic and discouraging, but I also remembered that everything is really the same; it is all for the purpose of helping the Sonship awaken. So I asked for help and I received it. In the moment, as I gave Him my mistaken thoughts, I received the Holy Spirit's true thoughts to take their place. Then later when I wrote about it, He acknowledged my discouragement and my fear that I could not retain what I was learning and that I would not be able to use it when the going got rough.

Holy Spirit: Dear one, it feels frightening to you because you are judging what is happening, and you are interpreting the event and your response to it. Let that go. Be of good cheer when you notice that your response to a situation is causing you pain. It is through your mindfulness that you are learning that you do not want to continue holding on to these thoughts and that you are giving yourself the opportunity to choose differently.

A good practice is to think of your story not as your "life" but as an interesting series of events that demonstrate the effect of wrong-minded thinking. You, dear observer, are watching these stories carefully as you learn which thoughts and beliefs create the effect you are experiencing. When you choose to bring suspect thoughts to Me and allow Me to correct them and bring them in line with your true will, you experience a different effect, one more to your liking.

As you allow Me to purify your thoughts, you begin to see the world differently. This makes for a happier life for you, which pleases the Lord Who loves you and wants only your happiness. It also helps awaken the Sonship, which is your only purpose and the true desire of your Heart.

When you notice the emotional effects of wrong-minded thinking, rather than be discouraged that this is still happening, rejoice that you have another chance to do the work. Be glad to see the thinking that indicates a mistaken belief in the mind, and be glad for the opportunity to choose differently by choosing Me rather than ego as the solution to this error.

Lesson 19

I am not alone in experiencing the effects of my thoughts.

The ego is all about doing. If something seems to be wrong, the ego wants to fix it on the level of form, because it gives it something to do. But the only way to effect true change is to make the correction at the level of mind. When I bring my thoughts into proper alignment I will have caused change.

Because there is only one of us, the change I cause is experienced by all. Bodies give the appearance of separation, and certainly we do not appear to occupy the same body, but our minds have no such gap. They are completely joined to make a whole. My thought does not have to leap to your mind; it is simply there, which is why there are no private thoughts. The belief that there are private thoughts is a shared delusion of the Sonship.

Since I share my thoughts with all, I affect all with my thoughts. Today I will be mindful of my responsibility, not to just the dream character, Myron, but to all of the Sonship. I will be vigilant for thoughts which bind us to the illusion and strengthen our belief in separation, and I will ask for correction. I will give myself moments of respite from the incessant chatter of the ego and allow my mind to dwell in the peace of God.

Holy Spirit, I have thought of many ways in which I can imagine myself as one with everyone. I am closer to feeling the truth of that, but I still think of myself as one person and everyone else as "other". Can You help me?

Holy Spirit: This is what we are doing in the lessons, dear one. We are walking that path one step at a time. It requires a lot of undoing, of emptying out, before you are able to accept this truth. You are much closer to this than you realize.

Truly all you have to do to change your mind about anything is to want something else more than you want what you have. The Course is designed to simply help you reach that decision. I know that you think you want to recognize your unity with everyone else, but I assure you there is still resistance or it would be done. Do not be frustrated by this. It will happen in a blink of an eye, and you will laugh at what you once thought was hard.

Me: I will have to take Your word on that one!

Lesson 20

I am determined to see.

Lesson 20 is another one of those pivotal points in the Course. It is a declaration of my intention to become fully awake. I am determined to see. I have set my goal and turned my footsteps in the direction of salvation. And what must I do to succeed at this lofty goal of saving the world? Today I must remember that this is what I want. I know from past experience that, as simple as this is, it is easy to "forget", because there has always been resistance to success, even though I say I want it.

Holy Spirit: Yes, dearest, you have been resistant, but never have you been so ready as you are now. Do not judge what may appear as failure this day. Each time you notice that you forgot to remember that you are determined to see, just say to yourself, "Oh, I forgot to do my lesson, but I am determined to see." This will be the truth, and each time you do this you will know it more completely. All of Heaven appreciates the effort you are making today.

Me: Thank You that I am able to hear Your Voice more clearly than I could before. Thank You for helping me with my part in the salvation of the world. I invite You into my mind and ask that you correct the errors in my thinking.

Fury, Vengeance, Attack. What Is It All For?

Lesson 21

I am determined to see things differently.

Lesson 21 has always been important to me because of the line that says, **"You will become increasingly aware that a slight twinge of annoyance is nothing but a veil drawn over intense fury."** Oh, my gosh, what a statement! I really believed that I could be annoyed and it was okay, that it had little meaning and that it was not as bad as being enraged.

At the local grocery store something happened to me that really drove this idea home. I was standing in line trying to get my groceries paid for so that I would not be late for something. I don't remember what was so important, but I do remember the lady in front of me who was engaged in a riveting conversation with someone on her cell phone. I was getting really impatient with her when I remembered this lesson. I decided to think about how I felt. What if I could feel anything I wanted to feel without guilt and without judgment? What if I didn't care how I looked or what I thought about myself?

Better yet, what if I could act on that feeling without any repercussions? I would not get in trouble or really hurt anyone, no matter what I did. I would just be expressing my hidden feelings, and that would be okay. I had nothing better to do as I stood there tapping my foot in impatience, so I really let my mind go. What I felt was absolute rage. Before I could stop my imagination, I had mentally grabbed that phone out of her hand and hit her on the head with it.

I couldn't believe how strongly I felt about this. I couldn't believe how strong my hidden emotions were. Never again did I doubt that annoyance is nothing but a veil drawn over intense fury. This is the kind of thing that encouraged me to become serious about being mindful of my thoughts, and to stop trying to figure out what any of it means. I just note if it is a true thought or an ego-thought, and if it is an ego-thought, I ask the Holy Spirit to help me see things differently. This has become my process, my path.

I remind myself daily that I am determined to see things differently. I pay close attention to my thoughts, and make every attempt to look at them with the Holy Spirit and to remain open to His correction. Having used this helpful process for a long time now, I know how effective it is. I know that untrue thoughts can always be seen differently. Maybe the ego-mind cannot imagine a different way to see, but the Holy Spirit will show me the truth, and the truth will always lead me to peace and to joy.

Holy Spirit: In making this your daily practice, you have invited Me to work with you in your mind, and you have made Me a part of your thought process. Each time you ask Me to look with you at a thought or a feeling, you make that decision again. This is your purpose, your salvation and your freedom.

Me: I thank You each time You show me a different way. My gratitude is never-ending. I love You.

Lesson 22

What I see is a form of vengeance.

Lesson 22 tells me that what I see is a form of vengeance. Here is an example of how I see this happening on a day-to-day basis. I have become identified with the body called Myron. I think that is who I am. As Myron I have a belief that there is only so much money in the world and that I must work very hard to get what I need. Because I am not really Myron, but an aspect of the Son of God, and thus have the power of creation, this thought, this belief, is instantly made manifest. Because I am a very good creator, it is a very convincing manifestation. I manifest it, identify with the manifestation, and believe what I see.

Now as Myron I live a life of hard work, trying to get my share of the limited supply of money. I compete with others for my share, always on the alert for signs that they are intruding on my claim. Is that contractor charging me too much? Is he trying to get my little stash of money? Is that company going after my customers, trying to steal the very bread from my mouth? How do I protect myself? How do I keep them from taking what is mine? They are attacking me and now I must defend myself by attacking in return.

As I become lost in this form of vengeance, I don't remember that none of this is real, that it doesn't exist at all. I don't remember that I set it up with my thoughts of lack and fear. I don't remember that I want to see it differently and that there is a way to do this. I am so busy protecting my little bit of money and giving all my moments to work so that I can have a little more stuff, that I don't have time to think about anything else. I have defenses to build, attacks to plan.

I will never succeed in feeling safe and having enough, because that is not the thought I identify with. The belief that created this life is one of lack, so no matter what I seem to accumulate, I will feel that I lack.

That is why I have been given the Course. I can, step by gentle step, back out of the bad dream I am having. These first steps are helping me to see what I have done and how I did it so that I can ask for another way of seeing. How do I know that I don't want this world if I don't see it for what it is? As long as I believe it is my salvation, I will continue to hold on to it for dear life.

I had a perfect opportunity to use this lesson. I experienced someone attacking me as a Course teacher. I see the Course as my escape from the dream, and I see my role as a minister for God as the way I make that escape. So this was a pretty big attack in my mind. It was like the enemy had made a direct hit at the center of my stronghold. It rocked my whole world.

I looked at this and saw how I was playing out the attack-defense strategy all over again. I was the innocent Course teacher just going about the work of my Father, and along came this vicious ego who tried to kick me out of paradise. Not my fault. I wasn't doing anything wrong. I was innocent. He was the guilty one.

I knew what to do about this. I would just forgive the enemy and everything would go back to being perfect. But that didn't happen. I kept thinking about it. I kept thinking how unfair this was. I thought about how wronged I was. Then I wondered if he could be right. Maybe I had built my house on shifting sand. Maybe I was kidding myself about what I believe.

Then I attacked back. I thought how very un-Course like he was. I thought how unloving his words were and how arrogant his remarks had been. Who did he think he was? I was so justified in my desire to defend myself. I should just set this character straight.

I was able to see this pretty clearly, and in the light of this lesson, I could see that what I was looking at was a form of vengeance. But I could not stop the flow of thoughts and my own return attack. All of this was taking place in my mind only, thankfully, but that did not make it any less destructive to my peace.

Me: Holy Spirit, could You talk to me about this please? I don't understand why it is that I can see what is happening, and yet I can't let it go.

Holy Spirit: Dear one, the depth of the fear you experience is not to be underestimated. Your great fear makes you desperate to prove your innocence. To do this you feel you need someone else to be guilty. You think you cannot afford to let your brother off the hook because you believe that one of you must be guilty, and keeping him guilty is your only hope of avoiding the wrath of God.

The fear of forgiveness has another layer. The whole ego thought-

system, which is behind the making of the world, is about attack. It is a projection of your fear and your anger. If you begin seeing everyone as innocent, the world will cease to exist. Then where will you hide from God?

Of course, none of this is true, and step-by-step you are learning to see all of this differently. You did not blindly accept the ego version of what happened on this day, and that is symbolic of your return to truth. The ego idea was still there. You see yourself in the world, and so you are always going to be aware of the ego thought-system. It is like a little voice in your head always demanding your attention. But you also were listening to My Voice.

The more closely you listen to Me, the fainter the voice of the ego becomes. It is essential that you bring the whole thing to Me. This is the way you look at it, and the way you allow it to be changed. Your part is to bring it to Me and to want the change. My part is to change it. This is what you have done, and that is what I have done. This is how the world will be undone.

Me: Holy Spirit, this is such a miracle. When I came to You, I felt like I had a constriction in my chest. It wasn't cutting off my breathing yet, but it was making it difficult. Now, just like that, it is gone. I feel like I have been released and am now free. I don't feel like my brother is guilty of anything. In fact, I feel love for him. I also feel like laughing at the absurdity of the whole situation.

That is a wonderful change. It felt so serious before. I also am grateful for the experience, because this lesson is now clear to me. Please help me today to become aware of those places where I am harboring secret attack thoughts so that we can work with them. I invite You into my mind to do this work.

Lesson 23

I can escape from the world I see by giving up attack thoughts.

"The idea for today contains the only way out of fear that will ever succeed. Nothing else will work; everything else is meaningless." That is a strong and uncompromising statement. What seems to be helpful to me is learning to recognize attack thoughts when I have them.

I was busy writing when I was interrupted by a knock on the door. My first thought was, "Shoot! Who is that?" That was an attack thought. I am learning to recognize even the subtlest of attacks, because this is the way I escape the world of fear and vengeance.

Another important concept introduced in this lesson is that there is no point in trying to change the world, because the world is just the effect and not the cause. I need to change my mind about the world, because that is where the cause lies. It is all about my thoughts and my beliefs.

Jesus reminds us in *A Course in Miracles* that everything in the world is a symbol of vengeance. I look at my body as it starts to age and see that I am having an attack thought. Age is attacking my body. Gravity is attacking my body. Bacteria and viruses attack my body. Other people attack my body. Everything in the world is an attack thought projected outward where I can see it. Fortunately, out here where I can see it is a good place for my attack thoughts. Through my awareness and willingness, the Holy Spirit can correct these thoughts.

One more important idea that is introduced here is that the effects of my thoughts of attacking, and my thoughts of being attacked are exactly the same. When I feel that I am being attacked, I am not at peace. When I am attacking someone, I am not at peace. There is no difference. I also remember that there is only one of us appearing as many. So as I attack any one of the many, I attack my one self.

As I am doing this lesson, I am feeling attacked. I keep thinking that I need to hurry. I am late for work. I have so much to do. How will I ever finish? I am being attacked by time, which, by the way, I made up just as I made up everything else in the world. Obviously I made it for the purpose of attack. So now that I am aware of the attack, I need to be convinced that I can let it go and that I want to let it go. I am willing to see this differently.

Holy Spirit: Good job, Myron. You are well on your way to freedom. You have given your willingness, and that is all I ask. Please remember that you are perfect and that you are completely loved. You are only releasing illusions that you imagined about yourself. You are not giving up anything about yourself that is really true. You are choosing to escape from something that is not real. In the end, you are only choosing to think something different.

Lesson 24

I do not perceive my own best interests.

The reason that I do not perceive my own best interests is that I am judging everything by my perceptions that are notoriously unreliable. My perceptions can change from moment to moment. Sometimes I will perceive a particular situation in several ways and be unable to make up my mind which one I'm going with. At my very best, my perception is just a perception, which is a way of seeing things. It is not the truth. Under these conditions, how can I expect the best result?

Fortunately, I do not have to depend on my perceptions. The Holy Spirit will interpret for me if I step back and let Him lead the way. The problem is that I am still attached to my own decisions. I still want to do it my way, even though I have proven to myself that I have no reason to expect a decision based on shifting perception to be reliable.

An unresolved issue for me is my job. I earn my living in sales. I feel very fortunate to have this job because it pays well and because it is challenging enough not to bore me to death, but not so difficult that it engages all of my attention. I don't want to lose my job. On the other hand, it requires so much of my time that I am unable to do as much with my ministry as I would like, and my ministry is what brings me joy. So I want a job that leaves me with more free time but pays good money. Holy Spirit, that seems simple enough. What am I missing?

Holy Spirit: Dear one, if you dig a little deeper you will see that you want more than you are saying. What else are you expecting from this situation? You feel like you do not have enough time to work on your book and that if you had another job, doing the book would be a cinch. So you are expecting a change of job to produce a book. In this job you have some challenges with personalities that you would like to resolve by leaving the job. So you want another job to avoid forgiveness. There are other expectations you are looking at in this situation. But, you do not perceive your own best interests.

You can attempt to run from the personal challenges of this job, but that will not really help you. You will still have the same forgiveness lessons in the next job because you are bringing them with you. What you really want is to be at the end of the lesson. You do not need another job to get there.

If you will step aside from your own faulty perceptions and your own faulty conclusions and allow Me to guide you, you will see that you don't have a lot of problems. You have only one problem and there is one answer. Your job is not your problem, and finding another job is not your answer. You have been carrying this conflict around for such a long time, precious one. Give Me that burden and allow Me to resolve this for you. You only need to release your need to do it your way, and it is done. Give Me only your willingness to allow it.

Lesson 25

I do not know what anything is for.

I gladly admit that I don't know what anything is for. I don't know what anything means. I don't know. And the reason I don't know what anything is for is because I give everything the purpose of enhancing my own personal life and meaning. This is obviously in error because there is no "personal". I am not an individual, not a body-mind-personality, not separate, not special. I am part of the Sonship. I am One. In believing that I have personal desires and needs, I am teaching myself that I am separate and therefore endangered, weak and vulnerable.

If I think about that simple pencil and say, "I don't know what that pencil is for," what does that really mean? In my mind I see pencil and I think, "Something to write my thoughts with, something to record my finances with, something to write my son's address with." In fact, pencil means something impermanent that can be easily erased and changed.

I have given all sorts of purpose to that pencil, some of it fraught with emotion, but it is all about my special needs. I need to keep up with how much money I have, which is about taking care of myself. I need to write my own special thoughts down, because they are mine alone and so very important. I need to keep up with my son, because he is mine and I have an important special relationship with him. I pick up the pencil and then put it down and walk away. I am saying to myself, "See, I am not the pencil. This proves separation."

I am being encouraged in this lesson to see that I have given meaning to everything based on proving and reinforcing the belief in my specialness and uniqueness; that is, I am supporting separation. If I will look at this with the Holy Spirit, with a willingness to see it differently, He will show me how everything is for my own best interests as I give up the ego's goals.

Holy Spirit: Myron, it is very tempting to think that if what you are doing in your life looks wrong in your eyes, that you must be making a mistake, or that you are falling short. Let me remind you that you don't know what anything is for. On the very deepest levels, you don't know what anything is for. In those moments when you are sure that you are wrong about everything, let Me assure you that I know what it is for. Place your trust in Me. I will lift you up. I will carry you.

It took me a while to understand how this message applied to the lesson. Now I see that the reason I often doubt myself is that I judge my reactions and thoughts based on what I think is expected of me. When I judge, I suffer. I am learning that everything has the same holy purpose, to help me awaken. As I let go of thinking that I know what anything is for, I am happy to be aware of it and happy to give it to the Holy Spirit, trusting He knows what to do with it.

Vision

Lesson 26

My attack thoughts are attacking my invulnerability.

I am invulnerable, but I am not going to believe this about myself if I have attack thoughts. The reason this is true is because if I believe I can attack, I believe I can be attacked. It naturally follows that I must not be invulnerable. If I am not invulnerable, I am not the Son of God. If I am not invulnerable, I am justified in protecting myself by returning attack when I perceive it.

"Nothing except your thoughts can attack you. Nothing except your thoughts can make you think you are vulnerable. And nothing except your thoughts can prove to you that this is not so."

One day recently I said something to my daughter. The look on her face made me think she took offense, but we were in a group and the conversation flowed and there was no comfortable way to get back to it. Later I thought about it and started to worry. I made a whole story out of that fleeting look, and before you knew it, I was attacked by her, had attacked her back, and in the end was crucified for my innocent remark.

Not one word was uttered between us, and I doubt that she would even remember the conversation. My attack, her attack, and all of the subsequent ill feelings took place in my mind. And it is only to my mind that healing applies.

I also see how yesterday's lesson applies here. I thought I knew what this incident was for. I thought it was for me to defend against. I thought it was for me to see how wrong I was/how wrong she was (couldn't really decide). One moment I thought I was insane; the next I thought I was supposed to set her straight.

It might simply have been a chance for me to allow healing in an area that I didn't even know needed healing. I see how crazy it is for me to think that I know what anything is for. I also see how my attack thoughts were attacking my invulnerability. It was a great teaching device. I feel grateful.

Lesson 27

Above all else I want to see.

Lesson 27 asks me to make vision a priority among my desires. Above all else I want to see. Jesus begins this by acknowledging the resistance we are likely to feel while doing this lesson. He answers our objections: What if we don't really mean it? Do it anyway, because it will bring us closer to the day when we will. What if it feels like it is a sacrifice? He assures us that this will bring us bliss.

When I first began the lessons, I was happy to see this one. It seemed to require so little of me. How hard could this be? I soon discovered that I had a lot of resistance that took the form of forgetfulness. I wrote the lesson on the palm of my hand because, even though I was resistant, I was also determined to overcome that resistance. Now I know that I want to see. This is my purpose, the reason I am here. Do I want to see above all else? My life seems to indicate that this is not yet my only desire; however, I remain willing that this should be so.

Holy Spirit, this forgetfulness seems to be a form of self-defense, or a defense against God. In forgetting to do the lessons or in forgetting my purpose in any way during the day, I seem to be defending my right to be separate. I thought that by now it was just a bad habit, but as I think about not defending myself, I feel tension in my body and a lump in my throat. I feel like crying. Can you talk to me about this?

Holy Spirit: That you feel this resistance so strongly is a good sign. In the past it didn't feel like an important lesson to you; you just said the words when you thought about it, and when you tried really hard, you focused on not forgetting. Now you are allowing yourself to focus on the idea that you really do want to see. You are even allowing yourself to think that you might want to see above all else. This is very good. Thank you for your willingness. This is all I need from you. Keep your willingness alive today by practicing this lesson as faithfully as possible. I trust you to do your part; trust Me to do Mine.

Lesson 28

Above all else I want to see things differently.

I continue with this lesson, only now I am becoming more specific, as I am determined to see something differently. There are several things of interest to me in this lesson. I am reminded that in seeing a lot of separate things I am not seeing at all. I look at my keyboard and think that it is a keyboard, therefore different from my Course book, different from my computer screen, and different from my fingers. I see only differences, and so I am not seeing. In learning to see differently, I am going to learn to see that anything I use represents all things because there is only one thing. All things are simply varying forms of one thing.

Another thing that is helping me is being reminded that I see only the past when I look at anything. Jesus is asking me to let that go. He is saying that if I will withdraw my perceptions based on the little I think I have learned in the past, I will see something beautiful. He says that under my ideas of what it is about is its real purpose and that it is the same purpose that it shares with all the universe. I feel a sense of excitement and anticipation. I, somehow, know this is true even if I don't have that experience right now.

Jesus is very gentle in this lesson. He tells me that it does not matter if I get this right away and asks only for my willingness to practice the lesson. When I first did these lessons, and for many years afterward, this lesson confounded me. I would stare and stare at my desk and see nothing but a desk. It looked exactly like the desk always looked. I could not undo what I knew about the desk so that I could see something different. So his reassurances to not let this concern me were really comforting.

I was having trouble with this lesson because I was using the body's eyes to look at the desk, and using the body's brain to process the information, and using the ego-thinking mind to do this lesson. Over time and with practice I began to realize that there is another way of seeing. Looking with the body's eyes is not seeing at all, but is image making. I think about desk and then my thought projects an image. I don't change the image by staring at it. To see differently, I must think differently. To think differently I must listen to a different voice. The desk as is was imaged listening to the ego voice. Can I take my metaphorical eyes from the image my thought produced long enough to change my mind?

Holy Spirit, at this place on my path I have no trouble accepting that none of what I see is real and that all things I see are images I made. I think of them as all the same energy, simply coalesced into different forms so that my finger and my friend's finger, my desk, and the sky are all the same thing and look different only because I want them to. I have come to this place by practicing bringing my thoughts to You with a willingness to see them differently, and I am going to keep doing that because it works. I know that I am not seeing the truth yet, and so not truly seeing. I am willing to move on to the next step in attaining true vision.

Holy Spirit: Don't become discouraged because more is not happening. Do not judge the results of your practice. When you ask Me to look with you, it is done. Trust that. I like your enthusiastic, open-

minded approach, dear one. That is so good for you, and I know that you, too, see it as a change in the way you have felt doing these lessons in the past.

And you are right that this has nothing to do with seeing with the body's eyes, though vision can change how you choose to image.

I assure you that your next step on this path to awakening is not in any way out of your reach. It is right before you, and you will take it as you are ready. It will wait for you as you set aside all your objections. Do you hear that little voice in your mind that says, "No, let's not do this," as you ask me for the next step? That is the ego voice that does not want to give up its creations.

That voice is not at the forefront of your mind anymore because you don't choose to believe it as you used to. This is the result of your practice. Continue your practice, be ever more vigilant, and watch for the subtle indications of ego thinking. Bring them all to Me, for I know what to do with them. Continue to invite Me to work with you in your dreams as you did last night, and don't worry so much about the meaning of the symbols you receive in your dreams. Your thinking mind does not need to understand. I love you.

Lesson 29

God is in everything I see.

Lesson 29 solves the mystery for me. God is in everything I see. Of course! This is why my keyboard can show me the purpose of the universe. God is in my keyboard. What a strange thought. It has to be true, though. God is in everything, so God must be in my keyboard. As I begin to accept the truth of this statement, I can feel myself begin to shift. Everything takes on new meaning for me. It sounds too strange to say that I love my keyboard, but I can say that I have new appreciation for it. When my fingers play over the keys, it is as if the keys and the fingers are somehow joined, a part of each other. I wonder if this feeling will persist?

Holy Spirit: Myron, it is hard for you to remember that everything you think of as the world is really just thought. Your mind wants to go back to seeing everything as real and each thing as separate from another. That is normal, so don't worry about it. You have already begun to doubt this, and even to accept, at least in part, that it is not true. Your understanding is growing, and so is your acceptance.

Remember that this lesson is about purpose. Everything you perceive in your life shares the same purpose. You can understand this, if you think of it in terms of asking what it is for. You already know that everything is for your salvation. You can look at your copy of the Course and accept that it is for your salvation. You can even see how an argument with someone can be for your salvation. But it seems strange to you that your keyboard is for your salvation. This is only because you see it as different, separate, and not the same as those other things. I am telling you that because it shares the same purpose; it is the same. Don't be distracted by the form.

The feeling you had about the keyboard was just a glimpse of the truth. When you know that everything you now see as separate is the same, and that it is for your salvation, you will feel such love and gratitude for all things that attack of any kind will be laughable.

Me: Holy Spirit, why can't I hold on to that feeling?

Holy Spirit: There is still too much resistance right now, but that will dissolve as you continue your work with Me. If you even imagined that your fingertips touching the keyboard right now were not really separate from the keyboard and got a real feeling for that, you would panic. You are still very much identified with yourself as a body and separate from other bodies and things. You are not yet ready to give up this identity.

Me: Holy Spirit, I see that this is true. If I think of my fingers as not being separate from the keyboard, I do feel very uneasy. I hate that. The things I am learning seem so clear in my mind, and yet I see that I am not entirely ready for them. Truly, it is depressing and a little frightening. Will I ever do this? It seems so far away right now.

Holy Spirit: Again, I tell you not to be concerned about that. All is absolutely perfect, and as I have told you before, you cannot do this wrong. As you have often said yourself, and rightly so, your salvation is a done deal. These concepts of time such as now and later, in the future, and someday, are just words. They have no real meaning. They are concepts that you use to keep God at bay. When you are no longer afraid of your Father and are ready to be embraced by Him, time will fall away with the world you have imagined, and you will see that you never left Him.

Lesson 30

God is in everything I see because God is in my mind.

God is in everything I see, because everything I see is an image created by my mind, and God is in my mind. God is in everything I see, because there is only God.

I know that the world I see is not real. It literally is not there. It is just an image, a picture of what is in my mind. I am projecting from my mind all the guilt that I don't want to acknowledge, in an unsuccessful effort to get rid of it. The thought of separation is not a creation of God and seems to be an attack on God. The idea that I attacked God is frightening and causes intense guilt. I push away the guilt by seeming to place it outside myself. Hello world!

But this lesson is telling me that there is something else in my mind. Behind all of the guilt I refuse to look at is God. So, instead of seeing the world as a reflection of my guilt, I can choose to withdraw my projections and allow them to be healed, and so see the world as a reflection of God.

I resist this only because there is something inherently scary about looking at guilt. That is why I projected it in the first place.

The part of my mind that set this protective device in place to begin with is terrified to see my defenses go. The ego part of my mind is still trying to defend against God.

The Holy Spirit in the mind remembers the truth and stands ready to lead me out of the maze of lies I have created as a place to hide from God. The way I do this is to look at my guilt with the Holy Spirit and allow Him to show me my innocence. In my innocence I will not need a scapegoat for guilt, and I will show my brother only his innocence.

It is good to remember that guilt comes in many forms: fear, anger, hatred, frustration, depression, unease, shame and doubt are some of the forms that guilt takes. It can be very subtle, and so I am vigilant for thoughts that do not bring me joy. I also watch for thoughts that place blame on others for how I feel, or place it on situations. I will keep looking with Holy Spirit at the guilty thoughts as I become aware of them.

If I look at my projections and see them as my salvation, then I am projecting to separate. Here is an example of projecting to separate. I lose a customer, and the thought that comes to my mind is that I have done so much for him, and now he is going to buy from someone else. How ungrateful! How unfair! I feel unworthy, less of a salesperson than my competitor, and I project those feelings onto my customer and decide that I feel this discomfort because of him.

I feel attacked, so I defend myself by returning attack. This ensures the continuance of the separation idea. I am here on this side with my own personal goals, my customer is over there with his goals, and my competitor is also separate from both of us with his own personal goals. I projected to separate and seem to have done so.

If I choose instead to look at my projections as opportunities to see what is actually in my mind that needs healing, then I am projecting to join. Same situation, but this time I noticed how I felt when I heard that I had lost this customer. I noticed that I felt anger, fear, and uncertainty. I began to doubt my capabilities. I felt like I had been attacked.

I remember that these are not bad or good thoughts; they are only true or untrue. I bring them to the altar and leave them for Holy Spirit who will purify my thoughts and return them to me. Now I have projected for a different purpose. Instead of using projection to hide from God, I am using it to awaken and return my mind to God.

Cause and Effect and Shifting Perceptions

Lesson 31

I am not the victim of the world I see.

I have several favorite lessons and this one is right there at the top. I am not the victim of the world I see. I can't think of the number of times I have said this to myself or to someone else. Even so, I find that as I do this lesson, I am appalled at the number of victimization thoughts that cross my mind. Let me stop right here and add a comment to that last sentence. My friend, Sonja, sent me a helpful reminder when she read this. Here is what she said:

> *In the beginning of our studies we "judged and then judged for judging", but as we grew, we learned that it was an error, not a sin, and simply noticed when the mind had fallen back asleep and returned to right-mindedness. It is an easy trap to fall back into, the judging for being asleep at the wheel, but what a massive relief it is to find we are innocent and need not judge ourselves.*

So let me say that I am surprised by how many victimization thoughts I found but am happy to give any judgment attached to those thoughts to the Holy Spirit to heal.

I am truly making a declaration of independence when I say that I am not the victim of the world I see. If I were a helpless victim, then there is where I would remain, because my happiness would depend on the world realigning itself to my liking.

I was thinking about how my kids persist in living their own lives the way they want to without any concern about how it seems to affect me. If I become upset because one of them is doing something that looks dangerous to me, I am saying that I am victim to their actions and that they are to blame for my fear. Since I cannot change their minds about how they live, this would leave me stuck in my fear.

As I begin to accept that I am not the victim of the world I see, I know that I am not a victim of my kids' lives. They are not making me fearful. They are just living their lives. I am making me fearful! All of the fear is in my mind. I am free to see this differently by giving the thoughts of doom to the Holy Spirit for reinterpretation, and this is something I can do. I am not a victim of the world; I have made myself a victim of my thoughts, and I can change this by allowing my thoughts to be healed.

The most important thing I can do with this lesson is to use it. In order for me to do that, I will have to be very vigilant against those thoughts which indicate that I am seeing myself as a victim of the world. The Course says to use it as a response to temptation. I will be alert to temptations to believe that I am a victim of the world, rather than a maker of the world.

Holy Spirit, would you please speak to me about this lesson?

Holy Spirit: Thank you for asking Me for My words. You do have a good understanding of this lesson, but as you have seen, it requires great vigilance to stay aware of the subtle ways in which you feel victimized. In order to hold the ego-built world together, it is essential that you see the world as not only separate from you, but that you see yourself as a victim to it. Releasing this idea will free you from the ego thought-system. This is a result about which you are still conflicted. You want to be free, but you are still afraid to be free.

The ego desperately wants someone to blame and will resist strongly any efforts to withdraw this blame and to see the cause of the world as yourself. This is the reason that it is so important to stay vigilant. Now that you are aware of the dynamic, the ego mind will have to find ways to place blame that are not so obvious. Invite Me into your mind today, and let Me help you see that there is no part of the world that is not a direct result of your thoughts. Then you will truly begin to see that you cannot be a victim of what you make.

Lesson 32

I have invented the world I see.

Yesterday's lesson taught me the happy truth that I am not the victim of the world I see. Today in Lesson 32 I am learning that the reason I am not the victim is because I have invented the world I see. I caused it to happen with my thoughts. It makes no difference if I use this lesson on what I seem to see with my eyes or what I seem to think. They are exactly the same.

I am glad that Jesus keeps emphasizing this because I know, for a moment, that I made the world with my thoughts and that it is not really out there, but in my mind. Then I return in the next moment to believing that the world is real and has real effects, and that I am its victim. I need all the reminding and practice that I can get.

I was especially interested in the last line; I have invented this situation as I see it. "As I see it" is important, I think. I can understand what that means as I think about a situation in my life. Yesterday I spoke of how I can see myself as a victim of my children's behavior. An example of this is when my youngest daughter moved with her partner to California. At first all I could see was a great distance between us. I could only think of earthquakes and raging fires that seem to occur there every year. I watched on TV as houses slid off cliffs in mudslides.

Because I asked for help, the Holy Spirit helped me to see that only in my mind was it dangerous for them to go. My mind was creating the danger. I had invented the situation as I saw it. They still moved to California, but I was finally able to see it differently and no longer focused on the danger but instead saw it as a wonderful opportunity. The situation remained, but the purpose I gave it changed. They loved it in California. They were very happy, and I was happy for them.

I asked the Holy Spirit for His thoughts on this and nothing came immediately, so I decided to take my shower. As usual, I first checked my weight. I was especially anxious about what I would see because I am trying to lose a few pounds by a certain date. As I stood on the scale, I remembered my lesson and reminded myself that I have invented the world I see.

I began to notice my thoughts about weight loss and this particular situation. I noticed that my ego mind was having a field day with this. I thought about how easily I gain weight and how unfair that is. I spent a few moments hating the fact that chocolate cake tastes so good and has so many calories. I would have been angry and resentful of my scale, but the little darling weighs light, so I was ok with that.

I thought about how unfair it is that so many people eat a lot more than I do but don't gain weight. I remembered, with resentment bordering on hatred (okay, they are really the same thing; remember Lesson 21), the *Reader's Digest* story about the woman who earned thousands of dollars overeating in competitions. She was so skinny that she looked like she would blow away in a breeze. Now where is the justice in that?

Suddenly, I saw what I was doing. I was blaming the food for my problem. I was blaming the world for setting the standards too high. I was blaming some innocent woman I had never met for making me feel bad by being skinny while eating a lot. I think that this is the answer I was looking for. The Holy Spirit was inviting me to see this situation differently. I had been looking at it through the filter of the ego part of my mind. What if I stopped doing that?

I began to think about how easy it would be for me to lose a few pounds, if I wanted to wear those black jeans to the conference. I know this is true, because I have done it before. I had been getting fearful because I say I want to lose weight, I know I can, and yet I choose not to. What is wrong with me? I reminded myself that I could see this differently. I choose to see that not succeeding at anything is a choice born of a thought. I can choose differently by thinking differently. This is so easy to do. It is just a thought. I can change my mind anytime I want to.

I began to feel very grateful for this situation. What a great opportunity to see that I invented this situation as I see it! The numbers I saw on the scale were just numbers, completely neutral in their meaning. Then I gave them a meaning that was upsetting to me. I changed my mind. I decided that this could mean something else. I could see that this was a simple problem with a simple solution and that it would be such a thrill to see my world change with my thoughts; I was looking forward to it. Now the situation appears very different. I have reinvented it.

The scale is still there. My body is still there. The black jeans are still there. The deadline is still there. But the meaning has changed, and it changed because I recognized that I had invented the situation as I saw it. I changed my mind, and now it feels entirely different. Thank you, Holy Spirit, for the clear and immediate example and for bringing it to my mind as You did. It was a perfect answer, as always.

Lesson 33

There is another way of looking at the world.

The idea for yesterday tells me that I have invented the world, and today Lesson 33 assures me that there is another way of looking at the world. It says specifically that I can shift my perception of the world in both its outer and inner aspects. If I change the inner thoughts, then my perception of the outer will also change to reflect this shift. My perception will always reflect the teacher I am listening to, the ego or the Holy Spirit.

In this lesson Jesus isn't offering us a magical solution. If I look in my driveway and see an old car and I think I want a nice new car instead, a brand new Honda Accord is not going to magically appear in my driveway.

Here is what I feel this lesson is telling me. One morning I wake up and look out the window at my old car. I think about how nice it would be to have a new car like my neighbor. Wouldn't it be nice if I knew that it would always start and that there were no pricey repairs looming on the horizon? I think about how I wish I had a new car.

Here are the implications in those thoughts:

- Implied in my thoughts is that my brother and I are different and separate and that I am in competition with him. Right now he is winning the competition and so I feel less than adequate, because he has a new car and I don't.
- Implied is that I lack, and therefore I believe in lack.
- I want a new car but not the new car notes, so I am conflicted as to what I really want.
- Also implied in this wish for what my brother has is the belief that my brother is more loved and provided for than I am.
- Another implication is that I am defined by what I own, that my self-worth is established by what I own.
- I believe that I could be happy, if only my car situation were different, which means I am a victim of this situation.

All of that is what I perceive when I look out at my old car. Clearly, I have given a lot of meaning to the old car. I have projected all of my doubts and fears onto that vehicle and made it responsible for these feelings. If I look at my car in a new way, will it turn into some other car? No, that is not what is meant here. Seeing the world differently is not a magic wand in which we manifest a different illusion. Jesus is talking about perceiving what is there in a different way, not changing what is there (though sometimes that happens).

Would having another car make me feel loved and protected?

Would it make me the winner, and would being the winner make me happy? Is my old car making me miserable? Is owning an old car the reason I feel less than and lacking? If I had a new car, would all my problems be solved? Buying a new car would change the way my illusion looks for a while, but because there was no change in the underlying beliefs, I would simply find another way to express those beliefs. For instance I might shift my attention from the car to how my body looks compared to everyone else's.

If I change my perception of what I see, then I will see the car differently, and I will see all of the implied perceptions differently. If I detach emotionally from the car, when I look at it I will see a piece of machinery. It will be something that gets me from here to there.

If I withdraw my projections from it, it will be a vehicle that works or doesn't work, that does the job I need it to or doesn't do that for me. I can choose to see the car in this way if I want to. There is no reason the car must be a status symbol. That is a meaning I gave it. I looked at the old car and felt less than. The old car didn't generate that feeling; I did. A new car cannot generate a feeling of well-being, but I can, whether I have an old car or a new one.

I think this is what it means to see the world in another way. The Course tells us not to seek to change the world but to change how we see the world. This doesn't mean we cannot have new things. I have a new car now, but I don't give the new car any meaning other than a reliable ride. It is not a status symbol or proof that God loves me. If I notice thoughts that signify that it has become any of those things to me, I can remind myself that there is another way of looking at this new car; it is not useful for me to give a new car that kind of meaning any more than it was useful to give the old car that meaning.

Holy Spirit: Dear one, you are right, there is another way to see, because there is always within you another Teacher. There are only the two thought-systems to choose from, two voices, and you are always choosing to listen to one or the other. If you are experiencing joy and peace, you are listening to Me. If you are experiencing anything else, you are listening to the ego-teacher. When you are unhappy, instead of trying to make your world look different, you have the opportunity to ask for another way to see.

When you look at a person or a thing or a situation, it may seem like there are many ways of seeing it, and this often brings you to a state of confusion as you wonder how to choose from the many. But this is the truth: there are always only two ways to see. It seems like many because there is one ego-thought taking many forms.

As you saw when you were thinking about how looking at an old car made you feel, there were many different thoughts that came to mind. But when you looked at each one, the feeling you experienced was not the peace of God. So they were just the same thought clothed in different words. When you asked Me how to see this, the answer brought you peace. You then remembered that peace is your goal, not having a different car.

This did not preclude having a new car. In the illusion there are things you need in order to function. You are not being asked to suffer in any way as you learn this new way of being. In fact, learning not to suffer would be a more accurate way of thinking of it. But you are also learning that your peace is not dependent on the world and that you can be at peace, whatever happens in the world. Is not that knowledge far more valuable than a new car?

I see that the ego voice can be distracting, even compelling. I also see that I can break its hold by being quiet for a moment and deliberately listening for the Voice for God. The more I do this, the easier it is for me to hear that Voice. Thank you, Holy Spirit.

Lesson 34

I could see peace instead of this.

Lesson 34 says this: *Peace of mind is clearly an internal matter. It must begin with your own thoughts, and then extend outward.*

I am learning to accept that in every stressful situation there is a peaceful perception, if I am willing to know it.

To apply this in my life today I must be willing to really look at my thoughts. As I was giving my five minutes to the lesson, I noticed that I was thinking things like, "I am worried about not having enough time, and I am concerned that I am spending too much money." But I also noticed a lack of engagement on my part. I was willing to note my thoughts, but unwilling to feel them. I was feeling very peaceful and happy this morning, and I didn't want to do anything to lose this feeling. In doing this, I am teaching myself that peace is a very fragile state and I could lose it at any moment.

What I did was go back and start over. First I asked the Holy Spirit to be with me as I did this. I know that if I try to do my lessons without His help, I am just fooling around with the ego and nothing will change except that I *will* lose my peace of mind. I thought about what it meant to not have enough time. I let myself feel the anxiety of thinking of running out of time. I did this with each of my ego-thoughts. I invited them all in for a little run through my mind. It is perfectly safe to do this with the Holy Spirit in charge.

I must have an active part in the process in that I must be vigilant for the thoughts, and I must look at them with the Holy Spirit, with a willingness to see them differently. This process is simple and straight forward, and I will keep doing it in a slightly different form all through the lessons.

Holy Spirit: Yes, this is a good process. This is exactly what I want you to do. Thank you for putting Me in charge. Thank you for being vigilant and willing. Do not be afraid of your feelings, dear one. It is in allowing yourself to experience these feelings that you will see what it is that is robbing you of peace. You will also see that it is literally just a thought.

You have another thought in your mind, and you are free to choose that thought, instead. In order for you to know that this is true, you must do it. So, allow yourself to feel the anxiety or other ego-induced feeling, and then choose the other thought, that you could have peace instead. Allow yourself to feel the response to the thought of peace. You will see that they are both thoughts, they are both in your mind, and that it is up to you to choose.

Me: Holy Spirit, I feel safe doing this with You. I am deeply grateful for this lesson and for Your presence in my mind.

My Holiness

Lesson 35

My mind is part of God's. I am very holy.

I begin this lesson by acknowledging that I don't believe this. If I did, I wouldn't need *A Course in Miracles*. Now that I have established this one thing, I have made it possible for me to begin changing my mind. As I do these lessons, I have learned to see "changing my mind" differently. I now recognize that I have a split mind. Part of my mind regards the ego thought-system as reality. The other part of my mind is as God created it. I am always free to choose the part of my mind I want to believe.

I can always know which part I am choosing by the way I feel. If I feel joyous, peaceful, loving, I am thinking with my right-mind. If I am feeling anything else, I am thinking with my ego-mind. It is no real mystery, and it is not difficult. If I tell myself that it is, I know that I still believe that there is some payoff in staying with the ego. That's okay; I don't blame myself or feel bad about it.

I just notice it and go on with my lessons. That is how I apply my willingness. If I begin to feel guilty or afraid of my errors, I know that I have chosen to view this error through the ego part of my mind, and I know that I don't have to. I can change my mind to the part that is God's.

This lesson is helping me to change my mind. Right now I think that I am many things. I have decided that some of them are good things. I like the idea that I am loving and helpful and kind. I like that I am a teacher of God. I like that I am a pretty good mom, and there are other attributes that I am proud of. I think that there are attributes that I don't like and am not proud of.

I can be arrogant and unfeeling at times. Sometimes I don't fit my definition of a good mom. I can be very fearful and often feel inadequate as a Course student. I sometimes feel self-righteous. In this lesson I am learning that none of these attributes, not the ones I am ashamed of or the ones I like, are true, because none of them describe me as part of God. None of them speak to my holiness.

I will not use this lesson as a way of overwhelming the ego-thoughts. I will not quickly replace "I feel inadequate" with "I am very holy." I don't believe that is the purpose of this lesson. This lesson requires that I be thoughtful as I consider what I believe about myself. I am being asked to be specific.

I will notice circumstances during the day in which I see that I am thinking of myself in a certain way, and I will realize that this is who I think I am. I will bring that thought to the light so it can be dispelled. My mind is part of God's. I am very holy. This is the light today to which I am bringing all errors.

Me: Holy Spirit, I have a lot of questions going on in my mind about this lesson. Could You just tell me what You want me to know?

Holy Spirit: Remember that you are not Myron/ego/personality/body. You are Mind/Christ/the Son of God. It is not hard to envision yourself as part of God and holy, if you remind yourself of the truth. As you said in the beginning of this lesson, you do not believe this right now. These lessons are designed to help you see what you DO believe about yourself and to change your mind about that belief. As you think about a specific situation and consider how you feel about yourself in that situation, you are given an opportunity to bring these thoughts to Me for correction. If you try to correct it yourself, you will just trade one mistaken thought for another.

When you look at this lesson through the ego, you cannot believe it could be that easy. You want to make it more complicated. This is the ego's way of maintaining itself in the face of simple truth, which will undo the ego as you allow that to happen. I assure you that you do not need to add anything to what I have given you. There is not something else for you to do. Just be aware today of the "I am" statements that you are making and thinking. Recognize that they are not true. Bring them to the Light for correction, and be willing to step back and allow it to be done. That is all I ask of you this day.

Lesson 36

My holiness envelops everything I see.

What I love about this lesson is that it establishes my sinlessness. It does so by pointing out that I am part of God, which means that if I am sinful, so is God, which of course cannot be true. This is perfect, unassailable logic. It also points out that if I am holy, so is my sight. It is my connection with God that establishes my holiness, and so it is my vision through God that is holy.

Vision is not to be confused with the seeing I do with the ego. Ego sight refers to perception, which is not about what I see so much as how I see it; that is, how I judge it. The Course tells me that I will perceive without what I believe within. So I am not looking out on the world and then deciding what to believe. I am looking in to decide what to see when I look out.

The world is a mirror, a perfect reflection of what I believe about myself. There has been a person in my life lately who has been a thorn in my side. I have tried to see her differently, but even though I have given this situation to the Holy Spirit, I continue to have the same reaction to her. As I was doing this lesson, I thought about her and decided to really look at what was going on. Maybe I can learn to see her with my holy sight, if I consider what it is that she is mirroring for me?

I first looked at what I see in her. She seems to be afraid of change and afraid of losing her status if there is a change. She seems very afraid of being judged. She thinks the way to keep herself safe is through trying to control everyone and everything in her environment. Ouch! She really is my mirror! I could say those same things about myself. I give my willingness to see both of us differently.

"Holy Spirit, I recognize these are error thoughts. I cannot be these things and still be part of God because they are not part of God. So, my perception must be faulty. I am seeing me, and by extension, her, in error. I am willing to see differently."

When I first started mind-watching, I was trying to change my thoughts as I noticed them. I would notice an ego-thought and would try to beat it back with a correct thought. I was missing the point. I now use this watching to let me know where I am in error. I then ask the Holy Spirit to help me see (perceive) differently; that is, I ask Him to show me another way to see this.

Jesus refers to this lesson, "My holiness envelops everything I see," as my protection and urges me to protect my protection. By this he means that I should continue my vigilance for my thoughts. By using this lesson indiscriminately, I am learning that there is literally nothing outside my holiness. I am learning that there is no difference between my body and the calendar on the wall. They are all in my mind and my mind is very holy, so everything projected from my mind is very holy. If I am not seeing my world as holy, I am not really seeing.

Lesson 37

My holiness blesses the world.

I am very holy, not because of anything I do but because I was created by God as an extension of Himself. I am very holy and it is the acceptance of this truth that blesses the world. How can my holiness bless the world? My holiness blesses the world because there is nothing outside of me. What I bless within my mind is blessed within the world, because the world is also in my mind.

As I was reading and thinking about this lesson, I noticed that the "thorn in my side" mentioned in yesterday's lesson continued to pop up in my mind. I kept trying to dismiss it as mind wandering. I was thinking about how this lesson applies to special relationships. I was thinking about how often in special relationships I have a "one or the other attitude". One of us gets our needs met at the expense of the other.

So I am thinking about all this trying to take it in and seeing how my "one or the other attitude" is affecting my relationships, and how I can get to a holiness attitude. But that woman, that thorn in my side, or Thorn as I will call her from here on, kept distracting me. She was like a fly buzzing around my face and just as difficult to shoo off. (By this time you are probably chuckling along with Jesus at my stubborn refusal to see the obvious.) Finally though, I did the mental slap on the forehead as I realized that my relationship with Thorn is a perfect example of this.

In my mind I had been having this "reasoned" discussion with Thorn in which I try to get her to see how wrong she is, and how right I am. I offer her all the reasons that this is true and imagine her weak rebuttal. Ha! She'll have to see it my way. She loses; I win! Okay. I get it, Holy Spirit. Now how do I move from this place of separation, and win/lose mentality? How do I get to "my holiness blesses" mentality?

Holy Spirit: Myron, you have taken the necessary steps. You have looked at what is happening. You have expressed your willingness to be corrected. And so it is done. If you notice that you miss being in the drama of win/lose and try it again, then you have merely given yourself another opportunity to choose again and to reinforce for yourself that there is another way to see. When you are choosing win/lose, you are making a choice for ego, and this is something you can do as long as you want to. What you are beginning to notice is that this choice no longer works for you. You do not entirely believe in it anymore.

So now you are learning that there is another choice. You can choose to become more aware of your true nature, to know your wholeness –

your holiness. Every time you make this choice, you are doing it for the entire Sonship, because that is what you are. The knowledge of your holiness spreads throughout the mind, and so the gift is for all. Your holiness does indeed bless the world because the world is in your mind, where your holiness is. You are only bringing it to your awareness, and so making it your experience, as well as your truth.

I was on my way to see a customer this morning and got a postscript from Holy Spirit. I was wondering how to perceive the war in Iraq. How could I bless this with my holiness? I considered my feelings about the war. When I think about it, am I feeling angry, fearful and hopeless? Am I experiencing hatred for those I see as responsible?

The Holy Spirit reminded me that I saw myself at war with Thorn. I saw her as having what I wanted and of trying to take from me what I have. I felt compelled to protect and defend and even to attack to restore my loss. Because in a moment of sanity I recognized that I could see this differently, I was able to choose God instead of ego and so was able to perceive the situation differently. I no longer feel that that she is my enemy and that for me to win she must lose.

Now how is that different from war in Iraq? Other than scale, it is exactly the same thing. I have an opportunity to see my brothers on both sides of the conflict as calling for love. I can see that they are all innocent and that no one is doing anything to the other. We are all joining, either in peace or in war, for the purpose of returning home. Just as the conflict with Thorn was only an opportunity to come to peace, so is the war in Iraq only an opportunity to come to peace. If I see it any differently, I am confused because I am listening to the wrong voice.

Lesson 38

There is nothing my holiness cannot do.

When I am in my right mind, that is, in my holiness, there is no guilt, no fear, no pain, and no separation. All is as God created it. All is whole. When I am in my holiness, this applies to all because I am all. Again, this is about choosing between God and ego. Both are in my mind, and even though only God is real, I am free to choose the unreal. In choosing God, however, I am in my holiness, and there is no separation.

Well (deep sigh), I don't feel like this is true right now. I don't feel particularly holy or whole. When the effects of choosing the ego in my life are manageable, I can be pretty detached, and I am able to see that all problems in the illusion have the same source and that source is in my mind. I can see that seeking to change the illusion (the effects) is not my purpose.

It is my goal to change my mind, and then it won't matter to me what the effects do. I won't care what seems to be going on in the dream, because I will recognize the dream for what it is and know that it does not exist outside my mind. It is just a figment of my imagination. Why would I care about something that doesn't really exist?

On the other hand, if I or someone I have a special love for is in pain, suddenly the illusory world goes back to being important to me, as it did when my son told me how sick he is. It is no more real than it was a moment ago, but now I realize how strong my experience of being in it is. In my pain all I want is relief. That is good, because it is motivation to do something, but I have a hard time holding on to the idea that relief comes from changing the cause and not the effect. It is all too easy to lose sight of anything except the effect. Because of my fear, I want desperately for Jesus to be telling me that it is in my power to change the illusions and that I am supposed to be working on that level.

I very much want my son not to suffer, and I don't want to suffer either. I do want the pain to go away, but I want it to go away because I woke up to the truth. Healing the belief in the mind of pain, suffering and death heals it for the Sonship, not just for any one aspect of the Son. Just recognizing this helps me to see how absurd the idea is.

If I ask for the healing of one body, I am asking that healing be made into a separation device that singles out a part of the whole for a special blessing. I am also asking for healing to teach that the body is real and in need of healing. How could that be true healing? What I really want to learn is that no one is their body and all healing is of the mind.

The confusion occurs because I want two diametrically opposed solutions. I want to affect the world, and I want to wake up and know that everything is perfect just the way it is. I can't have both. I cannot have two goals and expect anything to work. Is my goal to somehow fix things for my child, or is my goal to end suffering for all time as I awaken?

Holy Spirit: Precious one, I am not asking you to sacrifice the one you love for an ideal that seems far away from the reality of the situation. What you are attempting to do is healing beyond anything you can imagine on the level of form. You want only what is best for your loved one, but you are confused about what is best. There is in your mind the Answer, the Solution. Relax your hold on your fear, and bring your willingness to the idea of another choice. Even in this, you can see the Light. You can experience joy. You can be at peace. This is what it is for, to show you this.

Me: From past experience I know this is true, and I know that after I have done this, I will be so grateful for the situation that provided me with this opportunity for awakening. Once I have made another choice, I will wonder why I thought it was difficult. While I am still in the process of choosing, however, it feels so hard! It also feels very lonely. Holy Spirit, I am willing to know that I am not alone and that I don't need to make this hard.

Lesson 39

My holiness is my salvation.

If guilt is hell, what is it's opposite? This is the question Jesus asks us in this lesson, and it used to be very hard for me to answer. Now I understand that the reason for my confusion is that I didn't really believe guilt was hell. The Course says that I have an attraction to guilt and at first glance this seems ridiculous. How could anyone be attracted to guilt? And yet, as I watch my mind I see many instances in which I deliberately use my thoughts to invite a feeling of guilt.

I was in a hotel recently, and in the wee hours of the morning I walked down to the lobby for a cup of coffee. It was deserted and unnaturally quiet, and I started feeling creepy. What if some evildoer grabbed me? There would be no one around to hear my call for help. Suddenly I asked myself what I was doing. Why on earth was I thinking up disasters and focusing on them? The answer of course is that I am in love with guilt. I had just made some imaginary people guilty of violent acts. I had made myself deserving of attack.

The Holy Spirit is helping me to see that the world is a reflection of my thoughts, so it doesn't matter whether I see myself guilty or someone else guilty. It is all my guilt. My obvious interest in guilty thoughts invites more of them into my mind and soon I am awash in guilt. It all happens very quickly, so quickly that it seems to be happening to me, rather than by me.

But standing on the firm ground of my holiness, I experience my thoughts differently. When a guilty thought appears, I notice it and then allow it to leave my mind. I am learning not to give it my attention. I have not given guilt up completely, but I am more interested in letting it go than I am in feeding it with misplaced faith. Guilt has begun to starve from lack of attention. At least it's getting skinny.

As I continue this practice, something very interesting and wonderful is happening. I am learning not to take the thoughts in my mind seriously, and even to laugh at them. In the past it would happen like this: I would be experiencing a perfect moment. There was nothing in that moment to complain about, worry about, or regret. The ego mind would then dredge up a memory from the past that felt shameful. If it could not hook me with the past, it would invent some worry about the future.

If I gave this ridiculous parade of thoughts my attention and concern, the perfection of the moment would dissolve into pain, sorrow, anger, fear; actually it doesn't matter which of these because they are all the same. Guilt has appeared as a thought in the mind and if embraced as true, its effect is lack of peace. The story doesn't matter. The form of the effect doesn't matter. Lack of peace is lack of peace.

The funny part, the part that makes me laugh, is that I am beginning to see the absurdity of believing my thoughts. I have to ask myself why on earth I ever gave these thoughts credence. As I think about it, I laugh out loud! In the past, the ego would say, "Here's a reason to feel guilty." And I would dutifully respond, "Oh yes, I see. Give me another memory to reinforce that guilt."

I didn't use those words, of course. After all, that wouldn't be part of the game I play with the ego. In order to sustain the existence of the ego I have to pretend that I don't know what is going on. But now that I have chosen to break that incredibly painful and destructive cycle and to call the ego on its game, I am having a lot of trouble taking it seriously. Thus I am going around laughing like a loon at unexpected moments. I am innocent. I am holy. My holiness is my salvation.

My True Identity

Lesson 40

I am blessed as a Son of God.

Lesson 40 establishes my identity, and the next several lessons will help me to see some of the happy consequences of this truth. I am, indeed, the Son of God, and as such I am blessed. I do not always choose to experience those blessings and so need to remind myself frequently during the day that I can do so and am meant to do so.

I had an interesting experience with this idea. I was about to eat some really delicious ice cream, and I noticed that, as usual, I was feeling excited to eat it. At the same time, I was feeling guilty and fearful because of all the rules I have made up about the consequences of eating anything that tastes remotely good. (See yesterday's lesson about guilt!)

Anyway, the Holy Spirit suggested that I enjoy the ice cream. What a novel idea. Did He mean to suggest that I eat it with joy? I thought so and did just that. It felt so different than my usual way of eating that I laughed out loud. Ice cream tastes even better when taken with a spoonful of joy.

I have access to joy and to peace and love. I can experience any of these things any time I want to. It is just a decision. When I do this, I am deciding for God. I am also teaching myself that I am blessed as a Son of God.

Here is my favorite, the statement that I most want to be true for me all the time. I have a quiet mind. I am at peace. I am certain. I am joyous. When I think of these blessings, I see a mind that has become quiet, because I have stopped giving its endless parade of nonsense thoughts my attention. Into this mind comes occasional directions on where to go, what to do, who to see and what to say to them. Otherwise it is this lovely quiet place.

One of the surprises of this discipline is learning that the reason it has been so hard to quiet the mind is because I secretly enjoyed all its little dramas. As I finally began to achieve some degree of success, I saw these panic thoughts. Would I be bored? Who would keep me company? What would I do without thoughts to entertain and occupy me?

I read a lot. I read while I eat, while I wait for someone, when I am too tired to write, as I go to sleep. I drive all day as part of my job, and I listen to books constantly. Recently I was on my way to the store and reached for the CD controls. I realized I didn't have anything to listen to. It was only a short drive so no big deal. I laughed at myself as I reached for the dial several times on that short drive. I have taught myself that I need to be entertained by ego stories all the time.

So while I have finally gotten in touch with the desire for a quiet mind, I still have a lot of resistance to it. I was also afraid of a quiet mind. While listening to *The Teachings of the Inner Ramana,* received by Regina Dawn Akers, I heard something that further explained my resistance to the quiet mind. The constant thinking is my "I" self, my separate ego-identity asserting itself. When I stopped thinking long enough to become aware of what thoughts had been drifting in and out of my mind, I realized that it was "I" this and "I" that. I want some ice cream. I don't like that person. I think I would prefer to stay at a different hotel tonight.

Yesterday, as this happened, I stopped myself from the endless loop of mindless thoughts, noticed that it was the ego-self reasserting its authority, and chose differently by asking, "What would You have me do?" It was an uphill battle. I have given ego free rein for too long to make this an easy change, but it is simple and will inevitably be successful. I am blessed as a Son of God. I am very powerful.

I am not subservient to the thinking mind, only confused about what I want. It may not seem important to realize that I am using the mind to choose what I want for supper and to stop and ask, "What would You have me eat?" It may even sound silly. Why would the Holy Spirit care what I eat? But it is another step to choose to loosen my attachment to the "I" identity.

I am blessed as the Son of God. I am at peace. I visualize myself in the eye of the hurricane. All around me chaos appears, but in my Self there is only calm certainty. I know who I am. I am that I Am. Nothing that seems to happen in our story of separation can change that. I am still as I was created. Peace is my nature. Certainty is my nature. The winds of fortune shift and change and blow all around me but I stand in quiet curiosity, observing but unmoved.

I am blessed as the Son of God. I am joyous. I have always thought of awakening as very serious business. Awakening is very important, but I am beginning to understand that it does not have to be serious. I am beginning to realize what a strange idea it is that awakening to the only thing that is true requires my serious concentration; that awakening is such a fragile state that laughter and fun would shatter it. I don't know where I got that attitude, but I see that I was mistaking seriousness for firm intention. I am now firmly intent on joy.

Again, I have been surprised to discover a resistance to even this change. You would think that the idea of joy as a state of being would be so attractive that I would jump right on it. But the ego doesn't seem all that attracted to joy. I will be feeling joy, joy without a story attached, just joy bubbling up in me, and then ego starts throwing thoughts at me, thoughts that are designed to pull me back to its reality; thoughts of something worrisome or sad or potentially dangerous.

I have also discovered that joy is not really joy if it is part of a story. I can think of something happy that happened to me and feel good about it, but that is not joy. Joy doesn't depend on circumstances. So I can't think joy into being. The ego doesn't like this, because it is something out of its "domain". Joy just is, and to experience it, I seem to only need to want it and to not allow myself to choose something else instead. I speak of this in only the most uncertain terms, because I am on new ground here. But, oh my, what glorious ground this is!

Holy Spirit: Indeed you are blessed as a Son of God! I encourage you to choose joy often. There will be so many opportunities all day long to choose God. When you smile, Heaven smiles with you.

Me: What a wonderful lesson. Thank You so much. I am willing to be very aware of those opportunities. I am so full of gratitude this morning, Holy Spirit. Yesterday I began to feel anxious by the end of the day. It seemed that I was noticing the same thoughts all day long. I began to feel as if I was having no effect on my mind. But now I feel energized and ready to begin again.

Holy Spirit: Did you notice that, even as you rose from sleep, the ego-thinking mind was right there, beginning its process of establishing dominance in the mind? Its first thought was one of deciding if you should get up at that moment or go back to sleep.

Me: Yes, I noticed that. I noticed the back and forth play of thoughts of sleep versus what needs to be done today, how I have felt in the past when I got up early versus how I felt when I slept late and didn't get as much done as I thought I should. This opened a whole new line of thought creating doubt and uncertainty, and it began to feel confusing and discouraging. All of this in just a moment as I lay there. I never noticed before how burdensome all of this thinking is. I am encouraged, though, because I deliberately, and without thinking, asked what You would have me do.

Holy Spirit: I was hoping you noticed that. The ego judged the degree of your success yesterday based on its own interpretations. It cannot know if you succeeded, because it doesn't know what anything is for. After only a single day of concentrated effort on your part, you have shifted the ego dynamic. You began the day listening to the mind and very quickly chose to give your attention to Me, instead.

Today, when the mind seems filled with discouraging thoughts, just look at them. Is that what you want to believe? Looking with belief is suffering. It is not necessary or helpful. Look, instead, with mild curiosity. Then ask Me for My thoughts, instead.

Lesson 41

God goes with me wherever I go.

I love this lesson! But to tell you the truth, for a long time it was less of a promise and more of a desperate hope. I wanted it to be true, and yet my thoughts and feelings indicated to me that I did not believe it. Jesus knew that this would be true for us and says as much in the lesson: "We understand that you do not believe all this." He is so gentle and kind in his teaching. I pray daily to take him as my model.

While Jesus acknowledges that I do not really believe this, he also assures me that I can and will succeed, and that it is the most natural and easy thing to reach God. I think I must be getting closer to the truth, because the idea of God being with me is comforting and encouraging.

This lesson talks about separation and its effects. I see that the cause is the belief in separation, and the effects of this belief are worry, depression, misery, suffering and lack. But because I have believed that in separating from God I have sinned, it is intolerable to accept myself as cause. The world provides me somewhere to place blame.

I don't have enough money, a relationship goes down the tubes, someone I love is sick, and so it seems that the world is the cause of my unhappiness. Since I have cleverly made it seem that the world is outside me, it is easy to maintain the illusion of being a victim. Then I further obscure the truth by spending all of my life dreaming up cures for what I refuse to see as merely an error in thinking.

In reality, I did not separate from God. It is not even possible to do so, and so I don't actually have anything to be guilty of and nothing to hide from. This entire world is the effect of an error in thinking. These effects seem enormous, but in the end it is only a thought, and a thought can be changed.

This lesson is reminding me not to see the error as real and that, once I allow the error to be corrected for me, I can laugh at it. The world seems scary and deadly serious only if I believe that a false thought can have actual results. Of course, if I think I am here, I obviously believe just that, but there is a way out of this absurd situation.

The ego warns me not to dare take the world lightly. I am reminded of my grandmother warning me not to speak about certain things aloud or I would be inviting them into my life. The ego gives life and solidity to my fear of God through the nightmare world of war, abuse and disasters. I can go on believing the lie, or I can continue the process of letting go of the fearful consequences of believing in what doesn't exist.

I ask myself what I have to lose, and since I am asking my ego, it screams at me that I have everything to lose. It says that I will cease to exist. But the ego is not really me, anyway, so I don't have anything to lose by doing this lesson, and by frequently reminding myself of the truth.

Holy Spirit: Myron, you noticed during the meditation and again afterwards many ego objections to this lesson, many arguments against it. The ego will always object to truth. This is nothing to be concerned about. As you use these opportunities for the purpose of healing, you will become stronger in your choice for God over the ego. Here is something you can say to yourself when you are tempted to believe in the ego version of the world: This is just an effect of believing I am separated from God. It is meaningless, because God goes with me wherever I go.

Me: Thank you, Holy Spirit. I did notice that I seemed to be bombarded by these ego-thoughts, and it did feel fearful at first.

I appreciate Your support and Your helpful thoughts.

2011

Today as I read this lesson, I was not just hopeful; I was overcome by hope. I wept as I read the promise in these words. As I tried to sink past the picture of myself that I have believed in for so long I was aware of the objections of the mind. How can I believe them? These fear thoughts seemed to have battered back the Son of God and made him this small cringing thing. How could that be? How can I believe this? For a moment I can almost laugh, but for the tears.

Then I hear the ego's desperate attempts to pull me back from the brink, and I become afraid that these betraying thoughts in my mind will drive my true Self back into hiding. But can the Truth be so fragile? This could not be right. Who is this little self that prefers smallness and fear to greatness? Who is this little self who prefers to live in the narrow confines of its fearful thoughts? I am not that! "I am that I Am" fills my mind and I sob with relief.

"I am trying to sink downward and inward. It is quite possible that I will reach God." There, I wrote it. I said it aloud. That is what I am. Beneath the ungainly burden of separation beliefs is... God. I am that? Could this be true? Lightning has not struck. I don't feel like crawling under the bed and hiding. Who is it that has been afraid to believe the words? Who is it that is still afraid to claim his birthright? That little self is not "I". As the ego separation belief is sloughed off, is it God that will breathe me? Live me? Is this what I am hiding from myself? Is this closer to the truth of it?

The me I have always jealously claimed as my special self is melting away, dissolving under the brilliance of who I am. I feel this happening. But I also still hear the ego-thoughts bouncing around the mind. I still feel that annoying itchy place on my shoulder. I still want another cup of coffee. Something has changed, though. I cannot think of a single word to explain the difference. I am simply not burdened with the same concept of Myron that I had when I sat down, and I don't want another concept to take its place. I will just wait and see.

Vision

Lesson 42

God is my strength. Vision is His gift.

"God is my strength" is the reason I will ultimately succeed in spite of how unlikely this seems as times. I am not depending on my little ego-self, in which case, it really would be impossible. This is the reason I remind myself not to judge the appearance of failure on my part. My experience is that I am a body placed in time and space, and this experience includes all the effects of that thought. I get sick. I get angry and morose. I get frightened and also get excited and happy and in love. It all depends on the meaning I put onto each event. I fully experience it all, and yet I don't believe it. The appearance is meaningless. This self and this story are not who I am.

This is true, not just for myself, but for everyone. And this brings me to vision. Vision is how I will see when I know who I am. As I remember that my mind is part of God's, and as that more and more becomes the truth for me, I will look out on the world (which is really looking inward) and I will see not enemies or competitors, but only aspects of the Son doing what I am doing. We are all learning to remember who we are.

It may appear as if some people are bad or evil or against me, but all are just doing the best they can to return home to God. Some people's lives may seem like they are going in the opposite direction or may seem directionless, but their lives are their way home, just as mine is. Their lives are the way they have chosen to learn the lessons needed to help us all wake up. So there are no evil people and no enemies. As I realize the truth of this, I cannot condemn anyone, and I feel more love and compassion for them, as well as for myself.

Another idea that is very meaningful to me at this time is that

I am always in the right place at the right time and that my passage through time and space is not random. Absolutely everything that happens in the dream is a way to reinforce my separateness or an opportunity to allow that thought to be corrected. It is always my choice. Now that I have been in this dream for a while, I can look at the succession of opportunities and see how each one was perfect in the moment. It is like I was following a well-marked path that brought me from one lesson to the next perfect lesson.

I am committed to noticing the events and people around me and allowing myself to be aware of their innocence. This morning I went down to the hotel lobby for coffee. The employee who was setting things out was doing so with a cell phone tucked between ear and shoulder and so was moving slowly. When I asked where something was she told me breakfast was not ready now. I wanted to tell her to put the phone down and get it ready. She was the one who was running behind, and she was acting like I was rushing her.

I noticed my annoyance and remembered that annoyance is a veil over rage. I held my retort in and asked the Holy Spirit for another way to see this situation. The Holy Spirit showed me that she was trying to wake up, just like I was, even if she wasn't consciously aware of it. I didn't want to do or say anything to set her back. In fact, I wanted to do anything I could to help her. I cannot return to my Father without her. I wanted her to succeed as much as I wanted to succeed.

At the end of the day:

Hey, Holy Spirit, it's me again. Here is what happened today. It was the same, and yet it was different.

After that remarkable lesson and the journaling I did on it, I left the hotel and began driving from customer to customer. As I did my work, I watched my mind. I practiced my mantra. I frequently asked the Holy Spirit what He would have me do. This is the part that was the same as always.

The difference was in my experience of these things. I felt calm. I didn't get frustrated with myself when I noticed one of those magical reappearing thoughts. You know the kind: one of those ego-thoughts you notice and ask Holy Spirit to correct, and then, shazam, there it is again! Well, when that happened, I noticed it and reminded myself that I wasn't that. I am not the thoughts in the mind. I am not the mind. I am that I Am, and I am nothing else. It felt very peaceful.

I had a couple of moments when I felt tired of the vigilance and the practice. I asked for clarity and realized that if I was tired, it was not from the practice. Why would stating a simple truth make me tired? I was just experiencing resistance to the practice. I asked myself who was resistant. It is the mind that wants to think and wants to be believed. I am not that.

I felt expansive after the lesson and journaling this morning. When the thoughts appeared I felt like the mind was trying to shrink me back down to a manageable size. I visualized it trying to get me back into a box that it recognized. There were several familiar boxes, like the "what will people think?" one. It comes in two popular designs. The self-inflating "they will be so impressed with me" model; and the self-deflating "they will think me a fool". Actually, it turns out to be the same box, just seen from different angles.

I have to admit that I was a little tempted by the familiar box and briefly considered it, but it felt so good to be free that I chose against it. The mind didn't give up, though. It offered me all the usual options. There were a couple that were so ridiculous I couldn't even consider them when looked at from my new perspective. The thought arose that I should worry about a customer who hadn't returned my call. This is a variation on generalized anxiety, and I looked at it, but I was too vast and couldn't imagine myself squeezing back into *that* imaginary box. (It was so absurd to think of climbing back into the box, that I closed it firmly and slapped strapping tape on it, laughing all the time.)

Later the mind brought out the big guns. It brought me a memory of standing impatiently with my little boy as he tried to decide which pastry he wanted from the bakery. The clerk was trying to rush him, and I was siding with the clerk. Remembering this now, I thought what a terrible mom I was. The ego insists I should have helped my son, instead of making him feel inadequate that he couldn't decide. I felt so much guilt and regret that tears began to flow down my cheeks. I felt myself shrinking back to person size and felt like I deserved to be small again.

I so didn't want to give up my freedom, though, and I began my mantra. I did finally slip out of the mind's sticky grip, but it took a while. I gazed at the guilt box and noticed its sick attraction. At first I was afraid of it. Will I fall back into it in a weaker moment? But what is an awakening mind worth if it is so flimsy that it can't be trusted to stand up to the little ego mind.

I really do feel the strength of God this morning. My mind is quieter than it has ever been before, and I look forward to this day. What miracles will it bring? Surely, Vision cannot be far off.

Lesson 43

God is my Source. I cannot see apart from Him.

God does not perceive; He knows. I don't know, I perceive. God created the Holy Spirit to mediate between perception and knowledge. So I open my mind to the Holy Spirit and give Him my perceptions. He purifies them and returns them to me, much changed, much closer to truth. It is through this process that the mind is healed, the world forgiven, and the return to wholeness assured.

Me: Holy Spirit, I still feel some confusion as I read this lesson. Could you please help me?

Holy Spirit: The confusion you feel stems from the way you understand seeing. You still think your eyes see, because this is the function you give them in the illusion. Let's look again at what is actually happening. The mind embraces a belief and that belief is projected outward onto the screen of the mind in the form of a story complete with characters who seem to be living a life. Within this story, the characters are given bodies and these bodies have eyes that seem to see.

The character, Myron, looks through her eyes and sees what is happening around her. All of what she seems to see is filtered through the beliefs that created the story. The character next to her sees the same scene, but a little differently as she uses a slightly different filter. This is not seeing. It is perceiving what you want to believe, as if it were true.

Me: So people don't actually see something external to themselves, and what they seem to see is really a picture of their perceptions, that is their thoughts about it, their judgments of it? It's hard to hold this in my mind, because I slip from thinking of myself as the observer of this illusion to the character in the illusion.

Holy Spirit: Yes, I understand. But that is because you are using the ego mind to understand. As you learn more and more to relax the need to use your mind, you will experience the truth in a different way. You have already noticed this happening, but then you return to thinking for yourself, and the result is confusion.

When you look at a chair you "see" it in a certain way according to your thoughts about chairs. When you look at your friend, you perceive her in a certain way because of your thoughts about her, about yourself, about the situation, and about your own personal desired outcome to the relationship. God does not see in this way. He only knows, and knowledge is certain and unchanging.

I am the bridge that links the way you see with Vision. As you allow Me, I change your perception to bring it closer and closer to true Vision, that is, to shift your perception so that it is closer to knowledge.

You made perception for the purpose of seeing something that is not true. Now, with your permission, I am using what you made to bring you back to the only thing that is true. As you continue to ask Me to purify your thoughts, I will help you see differently, and your perception will become something so close to knowledge that the gap will be bridged.

Me: So, I cannot see apart from God because I cannot be apart from God. If I am seeing something that is not true, I am not seeing at all; I am perceiving. If I give my perceptions over for correction, my perceptions will become very close to knowledge, and then I will actually see. Thank You.

Lesson 44

God is the light in which I see.

Vision is not a function of the body's eyes. Vision takes place at the level of mind. God is in my mind and therefore light is in my mind. This is how I see. When I look with ego, I look through my body's eyes and see in darkness, which is not seeing at all. The mind (ego) is a small dark closet in which I imagine I keep the Son of God imprisoned. In it I surround myself with my thoughts, and believe I am safe and tell myself this place is the only place there is.

I have been practicing my willingness to leave that dark closet as I listen to *The Teachings of the Inner Ramana*. I have been asking the Holy Spirit to take me to the Heart, so I begin with that request. As I approach the Heart I imagine that it is becoming lighter and brighter, quiet and peaceful. I begin to realize that I am anticipating. This is the mind trying to think this experience. I let go of expectations. I will not decide what this experience should be.

I lay my concerns for the day on the altar and allow them to be taken, as I wait for the light to take me. I notice that mind is narrating the experience and laugh. I let go of the need to narrate. I notice discomfort in the body. Who is this body that experiences discomfort? I am not that. I notice frustration as thoughts appear and I am aware that, without realizing it, I have followed them. Who is it that feels frustration? It can only be the little self, the thought of darkness. I am not that.

I think of how I am going to word this as I write about it. Sigh. I don't need to plan this; I will be given words when I need them. I don't want the ego's words. I remind myself that I want the light. I want the peace and the restful silence. No one is forcing this on me. I realize that I have been experiencing performance anxiety. I want to do this right so I don't let Jesus down. This is silly, even for the ego.

It seems that I am still enamored with the little self I made to take the place of the glorious creation of Light that I am. I choose the silence and brilliance of God only briefly before I am enticed by the thinking mind to return to the dark closet it so prefers. But, oh, how lovely it was! I will continue my practice in patience and love. I am so much less attached to thinking than I was even a week ago. I am not nearly as afraid of annihilation of self as I once was. It is more than a lessening of fear. I feel the draw of the Light, the attractive pull of my Self.

Holy Spirit: Truly, precious one, there is nothing outside you, not even the body you imagine as yourself. All you think you see is imaginative play within the mind. It is not bad or evil, but simply not true. You are indeed ready to let it go. You have thought it into existence, and the way to let it go is to stop thinking it. This is why you have been guided to this practice. Do not be concerned by any residual resistance to this. Continue to choose the Heart, and the mind will simply dissolve in the Light.

Do not be embarrassed or ashamed of any of your ego-thoughts. Simply notice them and then give them to Me. They are meaningless unless you give them meaning with your judgments. Give them to Me and I will undo them for you. You are much closer than you think. Give me the thought that you are not going to succeed or that you are still far away from success. That, too, will be undone. Do not look at the seeming proof that you are not succeeding. It is a lie.

Me: Thank You for Your encouraging words and patient guidance. There are thoughts in the mind that say that the Light will remain forever just outside reach and that it would be much easier to just allow my attention to return to all my thoughts. But, honestly, I cannot do that. I have noticed how boringly repetitive these thoughts are. I have noticed how inane, self-defeating and ugly they are. I have noticed how unhappy they make me. It's too late to go back and pretend ignorance. Anyway, I may hold to some residual belief that I am my thoughts, but I will never completely believe that again.

Not I, But God in Me

Lesson 45

God is the Mind with which I think.

In the past I have approached this lesson with little hope of success. My mind has always been so busy; I have never been able to slow it down. Today, I read this lesson with a different mind. I am amazed at the beauty of it and the wonder of its promise. I have in my mind the thoughts I think with God. That is very far from my experience so far. Because of the practice I have been doing with these lessons and my listening to the *Inner Ramana* CDs, I am willing to consider that this experience could be different.

At the same time I notice that I still have thoughts of failure. I think about this weekend. During the weekdays I spend a lot of time alone and have a lot of reinforcement as I listen to helpful CDs. But without that advantage, my mind reverts to this busy highway of inane and repetitive thoughts. I see that I am only a child, a toddler, when it comes to letting go of my attraction to the ego-thoughts. I need a lot more practice and a lot of vigilance.

Still, I am willing to try; it is different this time, because I know that I will eventually succeed. I really wasn't sure that was true the times in the past when I had far more doubt than faith, but this has turned around. Also, I have had some small success in quieting the mind, so I know it can be done. I refused to think about what it would feel like to be aware of the thoughts I think with God, and what those thoughts might be. I want only to make a place for His thoughts to come into my awareness. The ego hates this, but I want to be surprised.

I'm going back to my practice of using the mantra and asking what He would have me do, have me say, have me think, in every moment. I will spend the week noticing the ego gibberish that passes for thoughts and remembering that I don't want to give it my attention. I will spend the week shifting my awareness from the head to the Heart. I am then going to try this exercise again and see how it changes.

Lesson 46

God is the Love in which I forgive.

God does not forgive, because He does not condemn. I remember the first time I read this in the Course and how important it was to me. I had, like most folks, grown up with the idea that, above all else, I needed God to forgive me. What a relief it was to hear that God knows there is nothing to forgive. I want this to be my model. No matter what anyone seems to do, I know there is nothing to forgive. It is through God's Love that I am able to do this.

It is through forgiveness, the recognition that nothing has been done, that I am saved. I have projected onto others that guilt which I saw within myself and could not bear to acknowledge. So that is why I forgive others. They represent for me my unforgiven self. I am never really forgiving anyone else, only my projections onto them. And so always, it is only myself that I forgive.

The ego-thinking mind cannot understand this. It believes that what it sees in the world of form is real and meaningful. It believes that it is only reacting to what has actually happened; in truth it is reacting to what it caused. The ego mind does not understand that the world is sourced by its thoughts.

Holy Spirit: You are correct that everyone you forgive is but a symbol of yourself, and so you have been forgiving yourself all along. You have noticed that your life is more peaceful and that you are much happier. These forgiveness practices are the reason for this. Have you also noticed that the more you do it, the easier it becomes? With practice you will feel even more motivated to continue it.

Me: I do notice that this is much easier now. I remember an early forgiveness lesson in which I was holding on to my grievance, even though I knew I wanted to release it. I said, "Holy Spirit, I know I need to let this go, but I am just not ready to right now. I am going to stay mad for just a little longer." It is funny now that I think about it. It was kind of funny even then, but I recognized the truth in it. I still hold on to some grievances more than others, and it is not always very important, just something little. I don't understand that.

Holy Spirit: Myron, these "unimportant" grievances are symbols of something else. It seems that you are trying to forgive a small thing, but beneath that small thing is a belief that you are not yet ready to give up. That is why it seems so hard. All forgiveness lessons are equal in value. Do each one as if it were your salvation, for truly it is.

Me: Thank You, Holy Spirit for that clarification.

Lesson 47

God is the Love in which I trust.

This lesson is full of such promise! I can already think of many instances in which I am attempting to use the ego thought-system to solve problems, and now I have an alternative. It seems like such a simple and foolproof plan, but I notice a resistance to loosen my "control" of the situation. The ego-self wants to maintain the right to make decisions, and I waver at letting that go. Lord, what am I thinking?

I remind myself of the wonderful promises in this lesson:

God is my safety in every circumstance.

There are no exceptions because God has no exceptions.

The strength of God in me is successful in all things.

There is a place in me where there is perfect peace.

There is a place in me where nothing is impossible.

There is a place in me where the strength of God abides.

I will remember that peace is my right, because I am giving my trust to the strength of God.

Holy Spirit: Myron, don't forget to choose God today. Each time you feel confused, angry or sad, anytime you feel anything except joy, realize you are depending on the ego, and choose God, instead. When you feel like you are running out of time, realize that the ego is running out of time, but you are not the ego. Choose to know that you are the Son of God, and there is no time.

When you are feeling sad about moving out of the house you have happily lived in for so long, realize that this is the ego re-experiencing the original sense of loss, the loss it felt when it chose separation. You are not the ego, and you can choose to experience this with God. Both of these thoughts are in you. If you want to, you can choose to do this entirely in the joy of God.

Remember, you may put Me in charge of the packing and the move, and this is the same thing as trusting in the strength of God in you. In this way you will not be anxious about all the details, because you will not be trusting in your own decisions. There will be many instances today that provide you with an opportunity to practice choosing the strength of God. Each time you make that choice, you become stronger in your confidence that you truly are God's beloved child, and not the ego-self you made.

Me: Holy Spirit, it is my intention to use today to become more aware of the strength of God in me. I ask that You help me with this, that You lead the way. I feel a sense of excitement as I think about strengthening my awareness of God in me. I especially appreciate the suggestion of putting You in charge of the move. I can be obsessive about details and put myself into a state.

Certainly, at the very least, I am giving up my peace when I do this. Now I understand why it is this way. When I obsess about the details, I am choosing to depend on the ego, which has no way of knowing what to do or when. Holy Spirit, as I say this, I am thinking that You are not interested in the illusion and changing the illusion. Why can I ask You to help me with my moving, which is clearly an illusional undertaking? I feel confused about this.

Holy Spirit: Myron, moving is part of the illusion, and you are right that healing takes place on the level of mind, so that is what we are interested in. We are using what you made to undo your belief in it. By looking at the beliefs, which made the illusion, you are given a chance to choose differently. So when you become upset that you don't know where to begin or upset because you think that you are running out of time, we look together at the belief that makes these thoughts possible, and you will be able to choose different beliefs. To change your mind you must first know what is on your mind. These little everyday moments in the illusion give you this opportunity. That is their value; that is what they are for.

Lesson 48

There is nothing to fear.

When I first started doing these lessons, I used this one to try to drown out the ego. I would feel fearful, and then I would inwardly shout that there is nothing to fear! In a sense, I was using the Course to stuff the unpleasantness deeper inside. This doesn't work. Just because I can't see the fear doesn't mean it is not there. It is still poisoning me.

Now I am looking at this differently. I see that the reason I am afraid is because I feel separated from God, and so I feel guilty and think I am going to be punished. But in truth, there is nothing to fear, because there is only God, and God loves me very much.

Right now it seems that I have all sorts of things that I am afraid of, and they all seem different from each other. I had so much trouble with plumbers that I keep expecting to have problems with them. Every time I come home I look around to see if my pipes are backing up or if I have a leak some place. I think about being nearer retirement age and realize that I have no plan in place for retirement, and it is way too late to put one in place. I am afraid of the future. I am afraid that my children will be sick, broke, have challenging relationships.

But no matter what form my fears take, there is only one problem and one solution. The problem is that I feel separated from God. The solution is the Atonement in which I forgive that error and realize I never left my Father. So now when I say there is nothing to fear, I can know it is true. I did not separate from God, He is not mad at me, and I am not going to be punished. Everything else follows from that. And yet, I know that I continue to be fearful at times and seem reluctant to relinquish fear.

What scared me the most was that I was afraid of my own determination to be in fear. I have not understood, but I am beginning to understand: if I identify with the illusion I make, the body/personality that I call Myron, I am going to be afraid to let go of the ego. If I believe that Myron is who I am and I think about letting that go, it feels like death, like annihilation. Now that I understand the source of my fear, I feel less panicky about my resistance. It makes sense now. I choose to look at my fear, recognize it for what it is, and allow it to be dissolved for me.

Holy Spirit: This is right, Myron. Continue your practice, as always. Remind yourself all through the day, when you are tempted to return your attention to the ego fear thoughts, that there really is nothing to fear. Notice each fear thought as it comes up, in whatever form it appears. It might look like anger or sadness. It will sometimes seem like others are responsible for your anxiety. Whatever it looks like, it is fear, and there is nothing to fear. There is no cause for fear because separation is not possible. You are just as you were created.

Me: Thank you, Holy Spirit. This morning while setting my

intention to hear Your Voice before I began this work, I noticed a difference. As I tried to quiet my mind, the ego-thoughts began to vie for my attention, as usual. At first I gave them my attention and felt the usual frustration. This frustration is the fear that I will never master my own mind. But instead of giving in to that fear, I chose to continue. I acknowledged the thoughts and then I sank below them. I reminded myself that I have a purpose and I want to fulfill that purpose. The ego is not my master, but my creation.

I remembered my commitment. I stated it in words; I intend to hear the Voice for God. I intend to follow only that Voice. I welcome that Voice. I have never found the words to describe what it feels like to be answered by that Voice, but it is a very joyful experience. It makes me smile and even laugh aloud, and the ego voice becomes very small. It makes me cry in gratitude.

Today I felt the power of my intention. I called this experience to me and I received it. Was it always that simple? I think so. I think it felt hard before, because in my fear of losing self, I was pushing against it. I feel like I am pure gratitude this morning, and I have to search my memory for fear, because in this state of gratitude there is no fear. I love You, God.

Lesson 49

God's Voice speaks to me all through the day.

God's Voice does speak to me all through the day, for that is Its purpose. Do I listen? My aim and my goal here is to hear the Holy Spirit. The ego voice stands in my way as I listen to its stories of specialness. The ego speaks often and loudly, and it is the practice of the lessons that helps me learn to tune it out so that I can hear the Voice of God speak to me. I think of this as the same thing I do when someone has the TV on and I am not interested. I just tune it out, and though it is still playing, pretty soon I don't hear it.

It is important that I remember that there are two voices in me. Which will I choose to hear?

One of the reasons I ask for Holy Spirit's message to me every day is so that I can practice going into peace and listening. It is not hard to do. I simply become quiet and desire to hear that Voice. The more often I do it, the clearer the Voice becomes. Sometimes I ask a question, and as I am writing I realize that I feel uneasy with what I have written. I know then that I have listened to the wrong voice. Wanting, really wanting, to hear the Voice seems to be what opens me to hearing the Holy Spirit.

Holy Spirit: Never doubt the holiness of what you are attempting when you listen for My Voice. I am always speaking to you, and so it is always possible for you to hear. But you cannot hear both voices at once. You must choose whether you want to hear My Voice or the voice you made to take Its place. Because you made the ego voice, you will be drawn to it. It is listening to that voice which reassures you that you are a unique and special person. That voice promises you that you are an individual and that you are safe from God, and it is that voice that tells you that you need to be protected from God.

All those times when you feel worthless, endangered, frightened, guilty or arrogant, are when you have chosen to listen to the ego. It tells you that in your specialness is your salvation from God, Who would have you be only the perfect creation of His Thoughts. He would have you know that you are One with All, while the ego would have you know that you are less than that. It would be impossible for you to mistake the two Voices, so different are their messages, except that you choose to make the ego your god and so believe it speaks to you of salvation.

Is fear salvation? Is guilt salvation? Only if you see hell as salvation could you believe the ego. Fear of God is an error in thinking and nothing more. Do not make your mistaken thoughts more than that, or you will be making them real to yourself. If you see yourself as vulnerable in any way, know that this is just a mistaken thought. Listen instead for My Voice. It is as easy to choose God as it is to choose ego. Both are equally available to you. I do not hide My words or make them hard to understand. If it feels like you do not hear them or understand them, it is because you still believe there is some advantage to remaining special.

Look for a moment at what specialness offers you. The ego offers you uncertainty. One moment it feels like you are better than the one before you. The next moment you seem to be less than this same person. There seems to be nothing that is stable and entirely dependable. You are in constant competition with everyone else in order to guarantee your place in the special order of things.

Conflict is the way in which you try to relate. Peace is just a word with no meaning. This is played out in every situation and with every person. The world of the ego offers an endless array of choices to keep your mind away from the one Choice. And yet, all choices of the ego lead you to conflict, to failure and depression. Where is the attraction of specialness when you look at it clearly?

What does God offer in place of specialness? While separation by its very definition weakens, God offers wholeness so that you will be powerful rather than weak. Separation leads to conflict and competition, while God creates only true communication, which inevitably brings peace. There is no conflict or competition in God, for there is only One.

Specialness offers endless conflicting choices with no clear idea of your goal and no way to reach it, if even if you knew what it was. God, on the other hand, offers perfect love and perfect peace. Which do you think will make you happy, choosing ego or choosing God? You answer this question each moment of the day as you choose the Voice to which you will listen.

Me: Holy Spirit, I want to hear Your Voice, and this morning as I prepared for this journaling with You, I asked that I would hear Your Voice clearly. I asked that all this day You might live through me. I offered this body as a vehicle through which You might express. I noticed fear and then I noticed that my mind began to wander to other thoughts. I recognize this as an effect of conflicted desires.

Holy Spirit: Indeed, your wishes are yet conflicted, my dear friend, but not nearly so conflicted as they once were. As the ego offered you the distraction of the world, you pulled your attention away from that voice and returned it to Me. Thank you. You felt my strength as words of reassurance and steeled your determination. In this way you set your intent to be the empty vessel through which God's Love might pour unimpeded. When you said that you wanted not to live this day, but rather to be lived, the ego felt self slipping away and tried to protect itself through fear and distraction. That is all that happened. Do not be discouraged because your newly strengthened desire for God did not go unopposed, but rather know that the opposition dissolves before the power of your choice.

Me: Thank You, Holy Spirit.

The day I first received this message from Holy Spirit was also the day I moved from my house to my daughter's house. I started the day with my ego, in a high state of anxiety. What to do first? How to get it all done in a single day? How to fit all my stuff into a smaller space and what to do with the stuff that doesn't fit? It all seemed so overwhelming and so important. I took a couple of hours out of my day to talk to my mind-healing partner, even though it seemed crazy to do so, considering all I had to do before the day's end.

It turned out that this was the best thing I could have done. In my friend's words I heard Your Voice reminding me that this could be a joy-filled adventure as easily as it could be a dreaded event. I began to see how blessed I am. I had my friend, Mary, packing for me while I worked, so that when we began the move, there was little for me to do with that.

I had friends from work come to my house and move all of my stuff to the new house. I barely had to lift a finger. My daughter arranged for temporary storage to hold the overflow, so I didn't have to do anything about that. She directed the movers where to put each item in the house, and provided pizza and soft drinks.

Truly, though I helped where I could, my only real job was to express the deep gratitude I felt to each loving assistant. I was also profoundly grateful that I was able to release the ego version of the day and embrace the miracle. Thank you so much, Holy Spirit, for being in my mind and for speaking always. I am going to practice listening, as this seems to be my part in the Atonement.

2009

This day, two years later, I am moving out of my daughter's house into my new house, and many of the same issues are presenting themselves. This year, though, I feel much more comfortable with the move. It goes more slowly, but it goes more gently. I am stopping more often to ask for guidance and to remember that this move may seem to be for the purpose of getting all my stuff from one place to another, but, as in all things, the purpose is my awakening; moving is just the form that awakening is taking right now.

Looking back on this two-year adventure, I see that where I remembered the purpose, there was a sense of expansiveness and things flowed effortlessly. Where I forgot the purpose and thought the purpose was to make something happen, there was contraction and difficulty. I am grateful for each moment of this time, for the lessons with which I was blessed, both those lessons which came easily and those which seemed difficult. When everything has the one purpose, the form is not so important. I am so grateful that God speaks to me all through the day.

2011

So here I am two years later again, and as I read the message Holy Spirit gave me in 2007, I am amazed at how meaningful it is to me now. It is as if it could have been written for me today. I have been spending time with the Inner Ramana, learning to hear *only* the Voice for God. I am learning not to listen to the ego, to the thoughts in the mind. As I do that, as I stop giving them my attention and belief, I make room for the Voice I truly desire to hear.

Yesterday I began to notice a painful tension between my shoulders. I asked the Holy Spirit how to see this. What He let me know is that the tightness was the result of trying to change my thoughts and trying to stop certain thoughts. He reminded me that this is not His intention for me. He asked me to notice when I am listening to the ego-thoughts and to give my willingness to simply take my attention from them. He asked for my desire to hear only His Voice.

As I did this, I felt the tension dissolve and the pain began to recede. Without realizing it, I had shifted from desire to efforting. I had shifted from allowing the transformation of mind to trying to do the transformation. It was a painful shift and I am grateful to let that error go.

Lesson 50

I am sustained by the Love of God.

I was very conflicted about this lesson when I first started doing the Course, and for a long time I remained uncertain as to how I was to use it. I understood that I do put my faith in all sorts of strange things, and eventually I understood that these idols were made by me to replace God. No matter how often they let me down, I would just keep looking outside myself for the one that would save me: the special man, the more interesting job, more money, being loved and respected. Such an endless list of saviors, and none of them was the answer.

I even understood that God was the Answer, though I wasn't clear about how that worked. I could see the path, though, and walked it. I still do, and though my understanding is better now, I still experience resistance to the Answer, often preferring the endless seeking of something outside me. I continue my practice, knowing that I am changing my mind. I can tell because I am peaceful more often than not, and that certainly wasn't true before.

Where I often got tangled up was when I tried to get rid of the symbols. I thought that to be saved I would have to quit taking medicine, quit caring about money, stop enjoying friends and being liked; but soon I was confused about where this ended. Do I quit wearing nice clothes because that would be putting my faith in how I look? Do I stop eating food that is good for me because that would be putting my faith in food, and if so, what do I eat instead? Do faithful children of God eat at McDonald's in defiance of the food chart? It was silly and yet it was also confusing.

What I began to realize is that I was suffering from "level confusion". Jesus was referring to mind level stuff in this lesson. He wasn't talking about what I do in the illusion, but why I do it. I had to remind myself that it is never about changing the illusion, but about changing my mind.

The pills, the money, being liked, the clothes, none of it matters unless I give it some meaning. Some people think being poor is awful and means that you are not loved by God. Some people think that being rich is bad and that you cannot go to Heaven if you are rich. In truth, money is just pieces of paper and means nothing until I decide what I want it to mean.

If I think I need money to be happy, I have made an idol of money and am using money to take the place of the Love of God. If I change my mind and place my faith in God, money becomes something I use in the illusion. I am not being asked to give up money (or anything else), but only to give up the meaning I have given to it. I am being asked to give up the "savior" value I have placed on it.

Me: Holy Spirit, I felt my blood pressure going up the other day and asked You if this was something I needed to see a doctor about. You said, "Yes." Then I said I didn't want to see a doctor for this and asked if this was something I could give to You. You said, "Yes." Can You talk to me about this?

Holy Spirit: What you have said yourself is true, Myron: that doctors are magicians and medicine is their magic. I was simply telling you that it is okay to visit a magician and it is okay to take their magic. It is equally okay to give it to Me, instead. I was saying that neither one was wrong, nor did I want you to make yourself wrong if you chose to see a doctor. If you choose to give Me your high blood pressure and are completely certain of your action, then you do not need a doctor. If you feel uncertain or afraid, then see a doctor.

Always ask yourself what this is for. The purpose of everything that happens in your life is salvation. As you look at your need to see a doctor and recognize that it is based on a desire to find salvation outside yourself and are willing to see it differently, then you have used it correctly. It does not then matter what you do. This is not about doing. This is not about changing the illusion. Wear whatever you want to wear. Eat whatever you want to eat. Just know that nothing outside yourself is going to make you happy. Instead know that your happiness is the result of knowing that you are sustained by the Love of God.

Me: Thank You for helping me to clarify this.

The other day as I was leaving a restaurant, I noticed a woman sitting alone at a table. Something about her defensive posture and the unhappy look on her face, coupled by the fact that she was eating alone and seemed lonely (at least through the filter of my own beliefs) made me think of my mom. Immediately I felt a wave of regret and guilt wash over me. I sat in my car in front of that restaurant and sobbed as I apologized to my mom over and over for not being a better daughter. Images of past transgressions, missed opportunities, and my selfish behavior flashed across my mind. When I could, I surrendered this to the Holy Spirit.

In today's lesson it says:

... let the idea for today sink deep into your consciousness. Repeat it, think about it, let related thoughts come to help you recognize its truth, and allow peace to flow over you like a blanket of protection and surety. Let no idle and foolish thoughts enter to disturb the holy mind of the Son of God. Such is the Kingdom of Heaven. Such is the resting place where your Father has placed you forever.

This is very much what happened for me in that moment. When I surrendered my ego-thoughts and interpretation of events to the Holy Spirit, thoughts came into my mind that helped me to recognize the truth, and I allowed peace, protection and surety to flow over me. Later when I got to the hotel, I talked to the Holy Spirit about what happened.

I was surprised at the intensity of the reaction to my thoughts and memories. I think I was confused about what this means, because the Holy Spirit told me that this reaction did not mean that any of the ego-thoughts about guilt and regret were true. It only indicated the depth of the beliefs I am still holding to. For this purpose, what happened at the restaurant was perfect, as it helped me to see what beliefs have made a home deep in the cave of my mind and still need to be relinquished.

Who would have thought that such awful grief would be cherished by the mind and held on to with such force. And yet, that is exactly what happened. I thought I had surrendered this guilt, and yet, here was irrefutable proof that I did not yet want to give up it up.

So again, I hold it up in front of me so that I can clearly see what it is that I am keeping. I ask myself if that is what I want. I remember that my relationship with my mom was the relationship she and I needed for our own awakening. I remember that seeing myself as a selfish, self-centered person who made awful mistakes that can no longer be undone is not truth.

These are the thoughts of separation that float around in the mind waiting for me to attach to them. Just because they are in the mind does not mean they are true or helpful. In fact, ego-thoughts are never true or helpful. That is why the Course encourages us to let them go. As we let go of the thoughts of separation, we make room for the thoughts we think with God. We let go of the thoughts of separation simply by not believing them. I had a bumper sticker that said: You Don't Have to Believe Everything You Think. It would have been more accurate if it said: You Don't Have to Believe Hardly Anything You Think.

Review I

Introduction

I love the way Jesus found a way to make the same points using different words. It makes it all new and fresh for me and deepens my understanding. I am learning that I have a split mind, which contains the two ideas: ego and Holy Spirit. I am learning that when I choose the ego thought-system, I am choosing against God and putting an insane defense system in place to keep God out of my mind. I am learning that the way to undo this is to look at it without fear and see what is happening. Then I can choose again.

Here is the sentence that really just blew me away: "And finally you will learn that there is no limit to where you are, so that your peace is everywhere, as you are." There is no limit to where I am. Jesus is not speaking to the little ego me that I made when He says this. That self is finite, fragile, vulnerable, and I know exactly the one spot in space where it exists. More accurately, I know the one imaginary spot in space where I pretend it exists.

Jesus is talking to my Self, which is unlimited, which exists everywhere at once, is everything, is invulnerable, and is love, is peace. The little ego-self seems to experience peace for only brief moments and then reverts to chaos, the idea from which it was formed. But that ego-self is just a wayward thought within the vast and holy mind that is Christ. It is meaningless. It is not that which I am. I am peace. I cannot ever, in truth, be without peace. I can only pretend for a brief instant in eternity that I am not what I am.

Lesson 51

Review

1. Nothing I see means anything.
2. I have given what I see all the meaning that it has for me.
3. I do not understand anything I see.
4. These thoughts do not mean anything.
5. I am never upset for the reason I think.

There is so much here that I hardly know where to begin. It is like being at a fantastic buffet and not knowing what to eat first. I think that I am going to concentrate on projection, because I need constant reminding about projection. I know that everything I think I am looking at, the world and all bodies (including the one I think of as mine) and every situation within this world are really inside my mind.

The reason I see these things outside my mind is because I don't want to acknowledge what is in me. I am afraid of what I have made and so I pretend it is outside me, and to fortify the idea I imagine an elaborate landscape and lots of "others" on which to project. Wow! How clever of me! Or so it seems. But because thoughts do not leave their source, I haven't really gotten rid of anything, and I am now further confused and frightened of what I think I have done.

There is a way out. I can look at all I see and recognize that it is merely a reflection of my thoughts and beliefs, and then I can ask the Holy Spirit to help me see differently. In other words, I want to trade my made-up thoughts for the thoughts I think with God. I want to take this way out. I have had enough success with this process to know that it brings me peace, which I have come to value.

I have noticed that my mind seems to revert to the old way of thinking, unless I am very vigilant for this kind of thing. For example, I begin to notice that I feel very frustrated that I cannot spend more time writing, and rather than look at the belief that generated that feeling, I begin to look outside myself for the cause of the frustration.

Here is how this works. I feel like I have too much stuff going on and am running out of time. I feel anxious about it. I decide that my anxiety is caused by the stuff that is going on. In my confusion I believe that I am the victim of my overloaded schedule and that there is nothing I can do about it. It is not my fault or my responsibility.

My projection is very convincing, but there is still a place in my mind that holds the truth, and I am never fully convinced. Something is not right, and I know it even though I am unwilling to face it, so I make more stories in a vain attempt to rationalize my behavior and justify my attacks on my brothers.

Even though this strategy is not working, I hold on to it. I notice that I continue to complain about the same issues and to make the same projections over and over. I seem to be so identified with this familiar list of complaints that I think they are who I am. If all of this is a product of my imagination, and nothing is outside my mind, then who is the "I" that I am talking about? Ooh! It feels like the sand is shifting beneath my feet!

Holy Spirit, I am willing to temporarily stand on shifting sand, because I know that this period of transition will be brief and that You will support me as I adjust.

Holy Spirit: The ego is your defense against God, and it would not be much of a defense if it did not leave you feeling confused and doubtful about your identity. But no matter how good the defense is, you are still exactly as you were created. You are not outside God in any way except in your imagination. You can imagine a separate "I" as long as you want to, but imagining it doesn't make it true.

You have experienced the pain you have caused yourself by identifying with the ego-self. You have also experienced the joy and peace that comes from loosening your hold on that identity. You are now moving steadily onward toward making peace and joy all that you experience.

The more often you make the choice for peace, instead of the choice for fear, the more certain you will be about your own true identity. And believe Me when I tell you, dear heart, it is a choice.

You are right that I am with you as you get your footing. As you notice each fear thought, ask that I look at it with you. I will show you the truth, and I will bring you comfort. That is My purpose and I am true to My purpose. I will never leave you. When you feel like you are alone, it is because you have identified with the ego, which is about being alone. The thought of wholeness is in your mind. Choose that instead.

Me: I am tired of making everything my enemy so that I can justify my anger and convince myself that my insane thoughts have meaning. I invite You into my mind this day, and ask that You help me see differently.

(Yesterday I spent the day noticing the stories in my mind that create and support the separate self-identity. They are many and varied. Each time I became aware of one, I would remind myself that the story is not real. I would say, "I am not that." That was really helpful.)

Lesson 52

Review

6. I am upset because I see something that is not there.
7. I see only the past.
8. My mind is preoccupied with past thoughts.
9. I see nothing as it is now.
10. My thoughts do not mean anything.

In these lessons Jesus is talking to me about how I have tried to replace reality with illusions of specialness. He lets me know that Heaven remains unaffected by my error but that it is certainly making me miserable. He also emphasizes that I can choose again, and that if I do, I can have Heaven back in my awareness. He certainly makes this seem easy, but I don't find it so. However, I am learning not to judge myself for my reluctance to give up specialness. It is much more effective if I simply notice it with a willingness to allow healing.

I really want the gifts of Heaven. I want peace and love and joy. But I also want the ego pleasures. I want to be special. I want people to look at Myron and say, "Wow, look at her. Isn't she a great mom? Isn't she just the best minister? Boy, I wish I were like her." Sometimes I'll settle for being the most victimized, the most pathetic, the sickest... it doesn't matter what it is as long as it sets me apart from others and makes me unique in some way. I cannot have Heaven if I persist in living in hell. Holy Spirit, please help me be aware of those times today when I am choosing hell over Heaven.

Holy Spirit: Yes, Myron, just notice the errors in thinking. Do not allow yourself to become upset when you recognize that you have once again chosen specialness. In choosing to be upset, you have made the error real to yourself and therefore harder to release. If the error is real, then it is sin, and if you think it is real, guilt becomes unavoidable. This is the ego's message, and it is the way you remain in hell. You are not guilty, but perfectly innocent. Because the ego-thoughts are not God's Thoughts, they do not exist, so you have never done anything wrong. There, you are innocent!

Me: Thank you for Your gentleness. I want to extend that gentleness to my brothers.

2009

As I read this review on another day, I realize that Jesus is helping me to see that I only think I see, but actually I am blind to the truth. What I call seeing is based on the past, which is not real, and so I am seeing nothing. I look around me and "see" different things. I see a tree that is separate from the bird that sings in its branches.

I see my daughter, who is different from my friend, who I also see. I cannot really be seeing what my eyes are showing me, because nothing is separate. I and the bird and my daughter and all things are the same. There is no separation. They are forms of the same energy. They are thoughts. I could think of what I see as thought-forms.

Then I think of this: how do I see them? I look at the tree and I "see" it (or perceive it) in a certain way. I might have a very romanticized idea of trees, a poet's vision of a tree. This thought of trees carries a whole world of concepts. As I look at the tree, I feel a smile form on my face. I see it as a thing of beauty, and as a home for the bird.

I feel some slight anxiety as I look at it and wonder if it will still be here after the next hurricane. I feel its vulnerability to weather, disease, those who would change its form to provide lumber or paper, and I identify with that vulnerability and feel afraid for myself. Now I do not see it as just a thing of beauty but as a victim, and by extension, I see myself as a victim, as well.

All that I see is based on the past. I see the beauty and the vulnerability, because I have ideas filed away in my mind that I draw on when I feel I need to. This is the ego's way of dealing with the world. It filed away stories and poems about the beauty of nature. When I see a large old oak, I look into my mind for the proper response and under trees this is what I find. And so I feel joy as I look at the tree.

There are some subcategories filed away in the mind. One of them is the picture of all the fallen trees after Hurricane Rita blew through this area. The mind compared the fallen trees to the original file and decided that fallen trees are bad. This led to another subcategory of greedy capitalists chopping down trees for profit and being valiantly fought by compassionate and concerned tree-huggers. All of these judgments were formed in the past by what I read, saw, was told, and decided to believe.

As I continue to look within mind, I see that the very form that

I call tree began as a thought in that mind. And even that was based on the past in which it was decided that separation would be an interesting concept to explore. Thus all of these various forms were created, each seeming to be different and apart from all others.

Jesus is reminding me of all this and reminding me that by seeing only the past, I am not seeing at all. I think he wants me to get my head out of the "filing cabinet" and release the past so that I can truly see. He would give me vision, if I would make room for it in my mind.

I am practicing quieting my mind through the use of mantras during the day, as I think to do so. I am practicing setting aside all "I think I know" and allowing the Holy Spirit to give me truth, instead. Instead of using thinking as the way I see, I am willing to allow knowing as the way to true vision. Knowing doesn't come from the thinking mind but comes when I take my attention off of these thoughts, which are all based on past learning, and simply allow the truth to be given to me.

Lesson 53

Review

11. My meaningless thoughts are showing me a meaningless world.
12. I am upset because I see a meaningless world.
13. A meaningless world engenders fear.
14. God did not create a meaningless world.
15. My thoughts are images that I have made.

These first lessons are the basis for everything the Course is teaching me. I am learning that everything I see is an out-picturing of the thoughts in my mind. It is like imagination on steroids. Normally I would think that to see in front of me what is in my mind, I would have to go through a long tedious process. I would write it down, hire actors to play it all out, film it, and then watch it on a screen. Even then it would be a two-dimensional representation of my thoughts.

But what is actually happening is that the thoughts in the mind immediately become the perfect three-dimensional representation that I want to experience. And I am not just looking at it, I am feeling, smelling, experiencing it. It is a true virtual reality. To get the full effect I quickly, more quickly than the mind can follow, forget that I am the source of my experience, and I really believe this is happening to me.

This amazing illusion is even more astounding as the mind multiplies it over and over a billion times, as if there were many different minds, each creating their own reality which is different from everyone else's. And because the source is quickly forgotten, each seemingly separated individual not only seems to experience its own private event, but also it is then interpreted, or seen from a perspective that appears different from everyone else's.

I am learning that the thoughts that create this experience are not true thoughts; they are not the thoughts I think with God, and so they are meaningless. This is the reason the experience often doesn't make sense and is, at best, unstable and often chaotic and upsetting. I can learn not to believe these thoughts and not to give them my attention. As I do this, my real thoughts, the thoughts I think with God, naturally come into my awareness, and therefore the experience of these thoughts begins to change.

Amazingly, the Course has to spend a lot of time convincing me that I don't want to keep these thoughts and this experience. My experience has been that I require a lot of convincing, and even as I have become certain that I am ready to do what it takes to return my mind to God, it requires significant effort on my part to remember that this is my desire. The mind continues to think its crazy thoughts, and I continue to give it my attention and sometimes my belief, even when the thoughts are clearly not helpful or true.

Though it takes consistent vigilance, I can let go of this insane and fearful world that I made with my meaningless thoughts by simply using the power of my decision to do so. The truth has gone nowhere. It is still in my mind, where it has been since God created it. If what I see seems anything less than beautiful and holy, I must be looking at an illusion, because it could not have been created by God. My real thoughts can show me something else because only what is created by God exists, and what was made by insane thoughts cannot take the place of reality.

As long as I look at the world and think it is really there, I will think that my problems are caused by the world, and the only way to help myself is to get some kind of control over my life. I have read self-help books. I have tried to get people to give me what I think I need. I have tried to get the world to be what I think I need it to be. Even my temporary successes have not brought me peace and happiness, so I try it again hoping it will finally work. Now I understand that this is never going to work and that trying to gain happiness by manipulating a world that doesn't exist is absolutely insane behavior, and I am ready to let the world go.

Holy Spirit, even though I am clear about what is happening and what I need to do to correct it, I keep getting confused about who I am. I keep forgetting that I am God's Son, and I return to thinking of myself as the ego. I know this is true because of the effects of wrong-minded thinking in my life. What is going on with this?

Holy Spirit: Yes, it is hard for you to hold on to the truth of who you are, but just a short time ago you had no idea that you could be anything but an ego. You did not realize that there was anything else to choose. Now you think often about the truth. You may not be able to hold on to it for long periods of time, but you are learning to value that identity over the ego-identity. You will keep what you value. The more clearly you are able to see how little value there is in specialness, the less you will want the ego-identity. It is only your value of it that keeps it in place.

Once again I remind you not to judge your apparent progress. Give Me your trust and simply do as you are prompted. Have you not begun to see how perfectly your path is laid before you? Each step is made possible just as you are ready for it.

Me: Yes, I have noticed this and I feel the perfection of it, and that is very comforting and encouraging. I have also noticed that the swings from sane thinking to ego-thinking are not as wild as they used to be. I assume that is because my desire for God is growing stronger than my desire for this experience of separation.

Holy Spirit: Yes, this is true. As you become more aware of your true desire, the desire of your Heart, you will place less value on the thoughts in the mind. As you place less value on them, you give them less of your attention and the mind becomes quieter and more peaceful, and this is reflected in your life.

Me: I know this is true. Thank you for reminding me. Please help me to notice when I am placing value on the valueless.

Lesson 54

Review

16. I have no neutral thoughts.
17. I see no neutral things.
18. I am not alone in experiencing the effects of my seeing.
19. I am not alone in experiencing the effects of my thoughts.
20. I am determined to see.

This lesson is about the power and direction of my thoughts. My thoughts may be meaningless, but they are very powerful. What I think without God cannot create anything real, but can make an entire universe in which I experience myself as attacked and attacking, fearful, angry and hurt. This universe is not real, but it is certainly my experience.

Everything I see as out there is really in my mind. So to know what I am thinking I need only look around. The world I see is a witness to my thoughts. As I made this world through my thoughts, I change the world through my thoughts. Separation is such a widespread and widely accepted illusion that I feel I must remind myself all through the day that I am not alone in anything I do, because I am not separate from anything. As I change my mind, I change every mind along with mine.

The way I change my mind is to desire the change and to be willing to allow it. As I bring each frightening and upsetting thought to the Holy Spirit, He helps me to see how I was misusing it to teach myself that I am separate and vulnerable. He corrects that thought and shows me that I am whole and complete.

I can't say this is hard, because I don't do anything but look with a willingness to see it differently. I resist, because I know that as I accept my wholeness, I am giving up my specialness. I cannot be an individual, unique person and, at the same time, be whole and One with All. My resistance tells me that I am not yet ready to give up my ego-self. But I am determined to see differently.

I had a good example of this a while back. I was on my way into a restaurant when I tripped and fell on my face. I was dazed and injured. I went to the hospital emergency room, and as I sat there I noticed my feelings. I was angry that this had happened to me (notice that I saw it as the result of outside forces causing something bad to happen). I was resentful of the long wait. I was in pain. I was worried about this interfering with my travel plans for the weekend.

I wanted to just leave but couldn't, because I was working when it happened and so would need to turn in an accident report. I resented that and decided my unhappiness was also the company's fault and resented them for it. I felt confused and upset that this had happened to me at all. I mean, why me? I'm a good Course student. Where the heck was my guardian angel, anyway? I really know how to create a world of convenient scapegoats for my every choice, don't I?

As I sat there vacillating between anger and self-pity, I suddenly had the thought that there was another way to see this and that I could even choose joy. I felt a little doubtful at first. How can I see pain differently and with joy?! But at the same time, I knew this was true. So I opened my mind to the possibility, and I can't say I became joyful about being there, but I did feel very peaceful.

The anger just dissolved. I enjoyed the time given to me to read my book. I took a little nap. I talked to the Holy Spirit about the fall and the fact that, once again, I was given the opportunity to realize what everything is for. I am very grateful that I used this mishap to allow the Holy Spirit to show me a different way to see. That is all it is for. I had used my thoughts to create a miserable situation, and by choosing to think with the Holy Spirit, I created an entirely different scenario.

Ego-thoughts (anger) are projected outward (sickness, accidents, etc), and are used by the ego to convince me that I am alone, at risk, vulnerable. This very same projection can be used by the Holy Spirit to show me that I am not a victim of a hostile world. This is done when I agree to see it differently.

Holy Spirit: Your willingness is your salvation. Remember that being determined to see does not mean to teach yourself to see. Be willing to consider that I am right when I tell you that you are settling for littleness when you decide for the ego. There is nothing little about you as you were created by God. You do not have to earn your divinity, for God created you Divine, and what God creates is eternally unchanging. Just be willing to accept what is yours as your birthright.

Later I received this message:

Holy Spirit: It is the belief from which these thoughts spring that is the cause. The individual thoughts can lead you to the belief that needs correction. Also, let Me remind you not to try to exchange one thought for another. Rather, allow Me to do that. That is My purpose. When looked at with the ego, you were brought low by a half inch of concrete pad. When looked at with Me, you became aware of another purpose and experienced the same event differently, as you realized that perception is not fact.

I felt so good about how this came out that I realize it was worth the temporary discomfort to learn this lesson. I am truly in charge and not a victim, because no matter what is happening, I have a choice to see it with ego or with You, Holy Spirit. The choice I make decides what kind of world I am creating. Thank You so much, Holy Spirit, for always being there speaking to me. I am glad that this time I listened.

Lesson 55

Review

21. I am determined to see things differently.
22. What I see is a form of vengeance.
23. I can escape from the world I see by giving up attack thoughts.
24. I do not perceive my own best interests.
25. I do not know what anything is for.

I love the perfection of the structure within this Course. This review begins as I set my intention: I am determined to see things differently. Why? Because what I see is a form of vengeance. Not to worry. I can escape from this world by giving up attack thoughts. I just remember that I do not perceive my own best interests, because I do not know what anything is for, so I need help. Just perfect!

I see the world as a blank screen across which images flicker, dancing in and then out. Where do these images come from? Only from my mind. I pretend I first see them outside my mind and then have thoughts about what I see, but my pretense does not change the truth. All I see is within my mind and all the dances are reflective of my thoughts.

During the recent presidential campaigning a friend told me that she was so tired of the conflict that she only wanted it to be done. It seemed to her to be an angry dance, months of attack and defense, getting uglier and uglier as we drew nearer the actual election.

For a moment I was confused. I found the whole process interesting, and I thoroughly enjoyed it. Yes, I saw the same apparent attacks and defenses that my friend did, but in this particular case my mind was not seeing it that way. The Sonship had joined in the desire to project attack and defense, and yes, I am part of that cause, but even so, I am free to interpret it differently. So, although I am one hundred percent responsible for the effects of my belief in separation, I am never victim to it. I am free to experience the effects differently and this is what I chose to do nearly all of the time that the campaign was taking place.

I saw thoughts of conflict, anger, hatred and fear being projected by our mind onto the screen that we call the world, and I was delighted to see it so graphically exposed. Only when we bring these thoughts out where we can see them and consider their effects can we choose to keep them or to release them. It was at this level that we chose the thought of separation, and it is at this level that we choose again.

There were times during the campaign when I would get caught up in the conflict. I would hear the ego-attacks and believe them. Then I would notice an effect of believing in attack. Maybe I would just feel heavy and listless, or perhaps I would notice my head hurting or maybe just a general dis-ease in mind or body. These uncomfortable effects drew my attention to my thoughts and beliefs. I could then realize that my mind was engaging in vengeance and that I was suffering for it, but I could choose differently. There was another way to see.

For most of my life I was so used to this kind of vengeful thinking that I actually liked the effect. I enjoyed being wronged, because it made me feel special. I enjoyed the attention that it brought to me. I enjoyed the flash of anger and righteousness that brought their own reward through the accompanying adrenaline rush. I valued these effects, and so I hung on to the behavior that created them. I thought this was serving my best interests. Obviously, I did not know my own best interests.

There is a limit to pain, suffering and sacrifice that anyone is willing to endure, and at some point I decided that I needed to find a better way. This is when I surrendered my belief that I understood anything. I do not know what anything is for. This was the beginning of true understanding.

Now I go through this process on a daily basis. Each time an unloving thought makes its home in my mind I have the opportunity to recognize that at this moment I do not know my own best interests, that I do not know what this is for, but that I have within my mind the Holy Spirit which does know. I can have the solution simply by wanting it more than I want to be right. Hallelujah!

Lesson 56

Review

26. My attack thoughts are attacking my invulnerability.

27. Above all else I want to see.

28. Above all else I want to see things differently.

29. God is in everything I see.

30. God is in everything I see because God is in my mind.

I was created invulnerable, but I can't see that because of my attack thoughts. I attack in my mind and then I see attack as if it were outside me, and I believe I am in danger. The danger is not out there, but as long as I deny the source as being in my own mind, I cannot see truly. I want to see. Above all else I want to see. I want to see differently than I have seen. I want to see without the projections of my fear being placed over the world.

There is a peaceful and loving world, because God is in everything I see. God is behind the image of the fearful world that my attack thoughts created. God is in everything I see, because everything I see came from my own thoughts, and God is in my mind. I cover that knowledge with my separation thoughts, but I am willing to see differently.

There is a person in my life whom I don't like. This is an attack thought. Each grievance is something to relinquish and none more important than another, because awakening is a total process. Put simply, I cannot awaken unless I bring everyone with me, excluding no one. So holding this one grievance is keeping me from my purpose. Holding this one grievance is keeping me in hell.

To make it easier for me, even in form it is important that I forgive. It is not as if this person is a casual acquaintance whom I seldom see and so am able to easily ignore, a passer-by in my life whom I will never see again. This is someone who is staying. Making it more difficult is the fact that others in this circle feel the same aversion that I do.

While talking about it with my daughter, we discussed why this is so because there does not seem to be a reason. This is interesting and, of course, the ego mind wants to come up with reasonable objections and justifications, but in the end this is not helpful. The only conclusion must be that I forgive myself my projections onto her.

So this is the way I am practicing it. When I notice I am judging her and seeing her as ego, I return my mind to truth by asking the Holy Spirit for correction. This is the way I forgive her, the situation, and myself. I have tried other methods, such as spending a certain number of days praying for her, which made a big difference, but then I began to notice that judgment was slowly creeping back in. Since there is only one mind, in truth, there is no one else out there; in the end all forgiveness is forgiveness of myself.

I hope this is the final and complete forgiveness. I am weary of having this judgment hanging over me like a guillotine over my exposed neck, for surely that is what judgment feels like. Holy Spirit, I recognize that my attack thoughts are attacking my invulnerability. Above all else I want to see differently. I know I can see differently because God is in my mind.

Me: Holy Spirit, I have tried to forgive on my own and have failed. I am ready to do an ego bypass and go straight to the Source. Please help me to see.

Holy Spirit: Thank you for coming to Me. Trying on your own was not a useless exercise, because it helped you learn that this is not the way to forgiveness. The ego is not interested in forgiveness. But within you is the answer, and I am the answer you seek. Simply give to Me the belief that there is value in protecting yourself from this person, and I will show you what stands behind the judgment you have placed on her. For surely, without the mask that judgment placed on her, there stands Christ, and there stands your Self.

Me: My mind whispers to me that there must be a fascinating story behind my belief that I need to defend myself from this person, and wouldn't it be great to know the story. After all it might help me give up the defense, or maybe it will prove that there is need for defense. What if she is truly evil and just wearing a face of innocence to fool everyone? Ha! The ego goes too far, and I recognize its insidious voice. The voice for separation is in my mind, but I don't have to listen to it, and I don't have to believe it.

Holy Spirit: There will never be a story that justifies attack. It doesn't matter how real the threat feels, or that it seems that your defense is directed outward and away from you, because, in truth, attack is always directed toward yourself. Whomever you seem to be attacking, it is you who forgets that you are invulnerable and thus forgets its own true Self. There is no way to separate yourself from your brother and no way to separate what you give from what you receive or, put another way, there is no way to separate what you teach from what you learn. Let your only desire be to awaken to your Self.

Me: Thank You. I give You my willingness to be corrected. I gladly offer You this special hate relationship and ask that You transform it into a holy relationship. I give my willingness to set aside my defenses and all the stories that I imagine will justify my need for defense. I want only to have my mind cleansed of all dark thoughts. I love You and appreciate You.

Lesson 57

Review

31. I am not the victim of the world I see.
32. I have invented the world I see.
33. There is another way of looking at the world.
34. I could see peace instead of this.
35. My mind is part of God's. I am very holy.

There are certain lessons that are touchstones for me. They are the ones I go back to over and over again in my daily life. One of them is Lesson 79, which tells us that there is only one problem and one solution. This makes awakening possible. I don't have to solve a billion different problems; I only need to recognize the one problem in each of the seemingly different situations.

"I am not the victim of the world I see" is another of those touchstone lessons. When faced with a situation that seems problematic, the ego's response is to project blame and thus to keep the problem. But I am not the victim of the world I see, and so, even if my first response is to project, I remember this basic truth and I must withdraw the blame. This puts me in a position of accepting correction. All of the lessons in this group are part of my daily practice. I know that I put myself into the position in which I now find myself. I know that there is another way to see it, and I can find that way when I ask the Holy Spirit for help.

I know that, no matter what seems to be happening, I could see peace instead of this. Sometimes that seems impossible, but the Course does not compromise the truth, and I don't try to negotiate with God. I could see peace, regardless of what is happening. Thank you, God, for that. And finally, my mind is part of God's, which is the reason all the rest is true.

My mind is part of God's. I am very holy. All answers are within myself. I don't need to look outward for a solution, though sometimes I do, because sometimes I block my own source of knowledge with ego-thinking. I am very holy. It brings tears to my eyes to think of it. I am very holy. I need to remind myself often, because only occasionally am I willing to see the truth of it.

I am reminded of the night that my daughter told me that she was thinking about reconciling with her partner. This was unwelcome news for me on every level, so much so that, thinking about it, I cried. So I let myself feel the emotions that it brought up for me, even as I applied these lessons to the situation.

First, I am not the victim of this situation, of my daughter, or of her partner. I am reacting to my own thoughts about these things. I am feeling the effects of the judgments I have about them. I am experiencing what happens when I am determined to bring the past into the present and, therefore, assure that I will experience the past in the future. So it is clear that I am not a victim at all, since no one is doing this to me, but rather I am doing it to myself. It seems that I am a victim to myself, but I am not, because I am free to change my mind.

I am taking a perfectly neutral event and placing meaning all over it. Then I believe the meaning that I gave it, and try to lock down my mind so that truth cannot refute my decision. To be certain that I don't change my mind, I listen to the ego's words of blame and guilt and project them onto Sheryl and Archie. This assures me that they are to blame and that I am only a victim. But I cannot be the victim of the world I see.

These lessons save me from unnecessary self-inflicted pain. To each ego-thought about the situation that comes into my mind, I have the same response: I cannot be the victim of this, because I have invented the situation as I see it. There is another way to see this. I could see peace. I know this is true, because my mind is part of God's, and so peace is in me; I cannot lose it or even be apart from it.

Me: Holy Spirit, as I give this situation, or rather my interpretation of this situation, to You, and as I remember the truth, I feel light and free and joyful. Then I begin to feel sad and resentful again. I don't want to bury my feelings, but as I look at them with You, I want to accept correction and let them go. I want to move quickly through this.

Holy Spirit: Thank you for your quick willingness to come to Me with this problem. Though you feel resistance to relinquishing the blame and the anger you feel, you are willing to do so; therefore, it is done. The sadness you still feel is the result of believing the ego-story and the only reason to believe it is because you see value in it.

You have been holding a grievance against Archie and have not chosen to look at it. [As Holy Spirit said this, I saw the exact grievance He meant rise into my mind.] *You feel like relinquishing that grievance is just more than you are willing to do. The ego-story you are clinging to is that this is just too much work, and why should you have to do this work. After all you are not married to him.*

Me: Ok. I am laughing at myself now. I see that this is exactly true. I also see that the form the relationship takes is not the issue. If I want to awaken, I must free Archie from the prison of my hate, because how can I go anywhere if I am busy guarding this hate to prevent his escaping it. I also see that I cannot go home, as long as I am separated from anyone, because wholeness is a condition of home, and judgment and hate are separation strategies. Even knowing this, I feel resistance to this forgiveness lesson. I need help.

Holy Spirit: Don't forget how much help you have, my friend. See yourself surrounded by loving friends who support you in this. They know how important this moment is, and they also know that you will succeed. Remember that the holiest of all the spots on earth is where an ancient hatred has become a present love.

Perhaps you would like to let go of the thought that this is very hard. That is, after all, just another ego-device for keeping you trapped in a prison of your own design. What could be simpler than returning to your true nature? I can assure you that there is no value in holding to this grievance and therefore no loss in relinquishing it. Think of some other grievances that you have chosen to release. Can you think of even one that you wish you had back?

Me: Now I know you are playing with me, Holy Spirit. If I wanted them back, they would be back. And no, I have never regretted letting one go. I also see that holding on to the grievance against Archie is not protecting me in any way. I am willing to let go of my defenses. I see that they are unnecessary. Please correct my thinking and heal my mind. I don't want Archie to be wrong. I don't want Sheryl to be wrong. What I want is to awaken. For a while there I simply forgot what it was that I wanted.

As I read the process I went through with Holy Spirit, I see that all the effort involved was directed at becoming willing to be healed. The healing itself occurred on an entirely different level. This healing, done without my help, is the miracle.

Lesson 58

Review

36. My holiness envelops everything I see.
37. My holiness blesses the world.
38. There is nothing my holiness cannot do.
39. My holiness is my salvation.
40. I am blessed as a Son of God.

I love the holiness lessons. I cannot hear that I am holy often enough. Thank you, Jesus, for these reminders. I am learning to feel my holiness. When I don't feel holy, it is because I have forgotten who I am. I have stopped listening to the Holy Spirit and have started listening to the ego. Again, this all about perception. How do I see the world? How do I see myself?

I met someone who evoked a strong emotional reaction in me. I thank that person right now for bringing up my stuff for healing. I kept seeing this person over and over again, and each time I would have this little feeling of annoyance. At first I denied it, then allowed it to be small, and finally I got honest and remembered that there are no small annoyances. I asked Holy Spirit to help me see this person differently, and then I rejected His help. I began to get a headache until, on the last day we were to be together, I had a migraine.

I just could not seem to release my grievance against this person. He had never done anything to me and, in fact, I don't even know this person. I just didn't like his ways, and the more I thought about him, the less I liked him. But why on earth couldn't I let this go? I think the headache was a reaction to the conflict I was in.

On the one hand, I didn't want to forgive. I was perfectly fine with my perception of this person. I couldn't for the life of me see him any differently than he "obviously" was. It was as if everything he did proved I was right about him and justified my thoughts.

On the other hand, I knew for a fact that this couldn't go on. I had to forgive myself for my projections onto him, and I had to accept that he had not done anything wrong, and neither had I. There was no question about this. My peace and my joy depended on it. The salvation of the world depended on it. So here I was trying to go in both directions at the same time. No wonder I had a headache. It was like a war was going on in my head.

I just kept going to the Holy Spirit with it, and He sent me an answer I could hear. My friend came to my room to share a forgiveness lesson that she was experiencing, and she read to me from the Workbook, page 401, "What is Forgiveness?" This is the part I found helpful: *"An unforgiving thought is one which makes a judgment that it will not raise to doubt, although it is not true. The mind is closed and will not be released."*

I guess that should have been obvious to me, but I needed to be reminded of it. Now I asked the Holy Spirit to help me see it differently, and I really meant it. I wanted my mind to be open, and I wanted to release my judgment. It was instantly done.

When I later told someone about my experience, and I said the words about this person that before had evoked so much negative emotion, I saw that now they had no charge whatsoever. In fact, when I thought about it, I started laughing. I couldn't even imagine why I ever cared about his actions. This healing was such a miracle. Every time the Holy Spirit does this for me I am so grateful.

In my forgiveness I recognize my holiness.

Holy Spirit: Myron, in that moment when you and your friend joined in forgiveness you stood on hallowed ground. A single forgiveness ripples throughout the Sonship, gently waking all the sleeping children of God. There is no small forgiveness. They are each of equal magnitude, and I assure you that what you did that morning was no small thing. All of Heaven rejoices with you.

Me: Thank You for your consistent and unfailing help, Holy Spirit. Thank You for speaking to me in a way that I can understand. Thank You for helping me to fulfill my part in the awakening. I rededicate myself to that purpose now. Where would You have me go? What would You have me do?

Lesson 59

Review

41. God goes with me wherever I go.
42. God is my strength. Vision is His gift.
43. God is my Source. I cannot see apart from Him.
44. God is the light in which I see.
45. God is the Mind with which I think.

These lessons help me to understand that I am part of God and that this can be manifest even in the illusion.

Each day brings opportunities in the form of problems that I have created through wrong-minded thinking. In each challenge I recognize that God is with me. He cannot be elsewhere, because He is in my mind. I think with Him, I see through His eyes. I cannot fail to meet this challenge, because He is my strength. It is only a misconception that I am outside God and that there is any other way that this could happen. This misconception convinces me that I can be alone and vulnerable. I only need to change my mind about this for the world of separation to fall away.

Holy Spirit: It is not useful to set your goal to change anything in the world, but it is helpful to use the world to learn that it doesn't exist. As you bring each problem and false thought to Me for correction, you are teaching yourself that you are not really in the world and that there is nothing out there for you to be in. You are learning that you are part of God and that there is nothing else for you to be part of. You cannot fail to reach your goal, because there is nothing else for you to reach.

Myron, I have said to you often that you are not the thing you see in the mirror. Think of the image you see as your avatar. It is only the visual representation of the ego beliefs held in the mind. It is useful to use your avatar to navigate the illusion and to use it to find your memory of truth. But it is not you, and believing it is you is the source of your fear and unhappiness. The belief that you are that image is the anchor that keeps you in the dream of separation. As you are letting go of that mistaken belief, you are learning to use the avatar for the purpose of awakening.

You are actually in God right this moment, dreaming that you are some place else. You often refer to that some place as hell, and that is an apt description. But the some place you are does not actually exist, except in your dreams, so you see you cannot really be there. You can think of Me as being your friend who is fully awake but visiting you in your dream. This is not literal, as there is only One, but it is a helpful way to see Me. Do you see how useful it is to have in your mind One who knows the truth and yet understands your experience as well?

I encourage you to continue watching your mind for mistaken thoughts and asking Me to correct them for you. This is how I help you wake up from the dream. I see what is going on in your life, and I know how you feel when these things happen, but I know it is all just a dream. From this vantage point I can reassure you; I can give you true thoughts; I can lead you back to your Self.

Your real Self sees truly, as it does not use the body's eyes to view the pale images you have mistaken for reality. It does not use the body's brain to "think", if that is what you want to call it. As you invite Me to guide you, to correct you, to heal you, light will come and you will finally see. You will see as God sees, you will think what God thinks.

You know this is true. Your mind holds the memory of God and of you as a Son of God. Turn to Me in your mind. Turn to Me often. I will strengthen that memory in you until there is nothing else in your mind. How we will laugh at the thought that you could ever have been this small, weak, frightened creature!

Me: I cannot grasp that memory completely nor hold on to it

for long, but I feel it. It is like it remains at the corner of the eye, there, but not quite in sight. In the meantime I continue to be vigilant and to bring my mistaken thoughts and my confusion to You. Something I notice is that when I am confronted by someone about something I said or did, I am often very upset by it. In fact, I can get upset in a way that is all out of proportion to what was said to me. Then I have a difficult time letting go of the fear this brings up for me. Can You help me see this differently?

Holy Spirit: The correction of mistaken thoughts is my job, and I will always do it. I will not, however, correct a thought that you want, even if you say that this is what you want Me to do. I listen, not to your words, but to your heart. It is possible, however, for you to change your mind about what you want. You know that this is true, because you have been doing it. Ask yourself what the belief is that is causing you to feel fear when others see you as wrong, and give me that belief to be healed.

When someone sees you as wrong, they are speaking from the ego, and when you respond with fear, you are responding from the ego. You are reinforcing the belief that you are both egos, and this will always induce fear, because the ego is the idea of fear. Your strength lies in God. You can turn away from that response by knowing that you are in God.

The ego always answers the ego, but you are not the ego, and you do not have to listen to that answer. You have within you the Voice for God, and you can listen to that Voice instead. As you make the choice to listen to God's Voice more and more often, you will no longer believe what you hear from the ego, and the ego response will become so meaningless to you that it will no longer illicit a fearful response. You can only listen to one voice at a time. Form the happy habit of choosing the Voice for God as the one you will hear.

Lesson 60

Review
46. God is the Love in which I forgive.
47. God is the strength in which I trust.
48. There is nothing to fear.
49. God's Voice speaks to me all through the day.
50. I am sustained by the Love of God.

I am at the end of the review for these lessons, and I almost hate to move on. I think everything I need to awaken is in these first lessons. What really jumps out at me in the review today is: I forgive all things, because I feel the stirring of His strength in me. These words really touch something in me, and I realize I do feel the stirring of His strength in me.

Forgiveness is what it is all about. For a long time I had the hardest time understanding the true meaning of forgiveness. My mind wanted to go back to the old meaning in which I condemned and then tried to pardon. What I understand now is that forgiveness is the undoing of that idea. Forgiveness is the realization that nothing has been done. It is easiest for me to think of each person as innocent; for some reason that word is more meaningful to me and brings me more quickly to forgiveness.

I am sure that I will be given many opportunities to see the innocence in everyone and everything. I intend to take advantage of each one to reinforce forgiveness as a way of life for me. Now that I have been doing this for a while, I am very uncomfortable with grievances, and I want to get rid of them as soon as possible. That is why it always surprises me when I hold on to one.

Holy Spirit: When you hold on to a grievance, it is because you think it has something to offer you. This is not true, and reminding yourself that it is not true will help you release it. It takes active work on your part to do this. You must stay vigilant to notice when you need to forgive, and you must become willing to change your mind.

What you do not think about is that while it takes effort for you to remember who you are, it also takes great effort to stay unaware. In fact, it requires so much of your energy to maintain the ego lie that you go to bed exhausted at the end of the day. Once you have forgiven yourself and have no more guilt, there will be nothing to be vigilant for and nothing for you to do. Being the Son of God is completely effortless; it is only the remembering of your natural state that requires effort on your part.

Me: Holy Spirit, I am also noticing that I can apply forgiveness to circumstances, as well as to people, and to myself. I have some circumstances that I want to forgive. I want to forgive the idea that there is danger in close relationships. I want to know that this is not true and to finally be free to allow the flow of love in my life to be unimpeded by blocks of any kind.

I want to forgive the idea that my source is the company I presently work for and that I dare not let that job go. I want to forgive the idea that working for God requires a financial sacrifice. I want to let go of the idea that there is anything to fear in following my heart, and especially, I want to forgive the idea that You, God, are mistaken in my abilities and that I will disappoint both of us.

Holy Spirit: My dearest, can you place these false ideas in My hands and allow Me to correct them? Forgiveness recognizes that they are not true, and forgiveness does not need your understanding and does not need your reasoning. These thoughts have created fearful images in your mind, and so many times you have clutched them tightly in your hands, while asking Me to take them from you. I will not pry them from your fingers, but if you will loosen your grip and allow them to drop into My waiting hands, I will take them from you.

You are afraid to give them to Me, because you think they are your defense against God. But I assure you, precious one, that you have no need for defense against your Father, who loves you completely. He does not ask for your sacrifice, and does not want your sacrifice. He wants for you only what you want for yourself. Would you be willing to want only joy for yourself? You are afraid to ask for so much, but there is nothing you cannot ask for. And so far, you have asked for far too little. Open your heart to My gifts; open it fully, and it will be filled.

Me: I don't know what to do. How do I open my heart? What will that mean for me? What am I supposed to actually do?

Holy Spirit: There is nothing you need do but accept correction. When there is action to be taken, you will be directed very specifically. I know that you are afraid of your ability to hear clearly. Your hearing is not deficient. It is your desire to hear that falters, and that blocks My Voice from your awareness. Even that is not something to be concerned about. The ego would have you feel guilty and fearful, but I assure you that this is not what I want for you. Guilt and fear are never appropriate reactions in any circumstances.

Me: I am reminded of Regina's message about asking and listening and knowing that the more often I do this, the more clearly I will hear.

Holy Spirit: This is true. Trust your Holy Self. This is a self-correcting process.

Me: I notice a tightness in my chest. Maybe I should work on one thing at a time. Maybe it is too much to take on relationships and my job at the same time.

Holy Spirit: They are the same problem. Don't think of them as separate issues. Relax about this, Myron. You are not being asked to do anything you don't want to do. This is what you want. The transition from fearful thinking to joyful acceptance will be seamless, as you relax and allow.

Me: I am willing to accept Your healing, Holy Spirit. I am willing to await Your instructions. I am willing to release my idea of what this should look like. I am willing to allow it to unfold naturally. I love You.

2011

I have experienced forgiveness of some long-held grievances. Here is what I did to forgive.

I became unwilling to hold a grievance.

What happened:

I looked at the individuals involved and felt my heart fill with love and gratitude.

Amazing! Who would have thought it could be so easy to be happy.

Lesson 61

I am the light of the world.

I don't always feel like the light of the world. But I no longer feel arrogant when I say it. I do understand that it is true about me, even if I don't fully understand what it means or even what it is supposed to look like. Jesus is helping me to understand that this is my natural state and that it is not arrogant to accept myself as God created me.

It is only arrogant if I misunderstand it and assume that I am different and better than others whom I mistakenly believe are not the light of the world. Understanding it correctly, I know I am not the ego and a separated person different than my brother. "I" in his case is all-inclusive. We, as one, are all the light of the world and it is my function to know this.

More and more my life is such a joy. I have a purpose in this life, and I know my purpose. I love and am loved. I am beginning to understand what it means to be God's Son… not there yet, but beginning. On the other hand, sometimes I forget everything and am right back in the ego thought-system. I don't remember what was going on in my dreams last night, but I woke up feeling anxious and not much like a child of God.

When I opened my book and saw the lesson, my first thought was, "Oh no, I can't relate to that today." I felt more like the darkness of the world; in fact, Jesus recognizes that this is how we think of ourselves, and that is why we need these lessons. This is not something that just happens. It is a process. If it weren't, there would be one lesson instead of 365 of them.

There was a time in my life when I would have stayed with this feeling for a long time, but I can no longer tolerate a loss of peace. I invited Jesus to sit with me as I experienced this fully, allowing myself to feel the upset, the fear, the anger, the sadness, every emotion that comes with the thoughts and beliefs that brought this on. I let myself really look at this, knowing that I was not alone, that Jesus was with me. I invited Him to correct my thinking, and I felt the clouds begin to lift. Finally, I was able to say the words, "I am the Light of the world."

As I continue my day, I am committed to remaining a light, a symbol of what we are meant to be. As I do this for myself, I do it for all, because there is only One.

Me: I am feeling such gratitude, Holy Spirit, for the healing I experienced this morning. It was exactly as Jesus said it would be. I looked at it with You and was willing to see it differently, and You did the rest. Thank You so much.

Holy Spirit: Myron, We are grateful to you for having the faith to step out of the ego long enough to ask for help. Each time you do this, you are teaching yourself that separation is not what you want. We also understand that it is not always easy to do this, because you are by no means entirely convinced that you don't want to be separate.

You still value your specialness, but this morning you willingly set it aside and accepted wholeness, instead. As you continue to do this, you will learn to value what is truly valuable, and when you no longer value anything else, you will no longer be aware of anything else. It sometimes feels difficult now, but it is truly that simple. It is only your value of separation that keeps it in place within your mind.

Do you notice, Myron, how much simpler this is when you do your part and then step aside and allow Me to do Mine? The process becomes confused when you try to psychoanalyze and work out what needs to change to make things right. That is the ego trying to join in the process, and that is not helpful. Stick with the experience of your feelings, and notice your thoughts with a willingness to change your mind. Aside from that, you need do nothing. I will do the rest, just as I did this morning. Thank you for your willingness to let that happen.

2011

My acceptance of myself as the light of the world has shifted. I am not as hesitant to embrace my truth as I was just last year. I think the most significant change is that now I don't stop thinking of myself as the light of the world, just because I sometimes stop acting like it. As long as I believe, even a little, the ego-thoughts in my mind, I will sometimes become confused. But now I never believe I am my confusion. That is no small thing, and I am so grateful.

Lesson 62

Forgiveness is my function as the light of the world.

Forgiveness is my function in every circumstance. For this to be meaningful the emphasis must be on the word "every". I cannot set any person or circumstance aside from forgiveness and still be fulfilling my function. Two things really stand out to me. One is that illusions about myself and illusions about the world are all the same. So, as I forgive the world, I forgive myself. Forgiveness of anyone or anything is my salvation.

The second thing that stood out to me is that when I attack, I am making other things separate and therefore making myself weak, and so will feel vulnerable and small. When I forgive, I am calling on the Christ within me and so will feel my strength and power. I will be restored to the invulnerable state in which I was created.

Before I can apply forgiveness in my life, I must truly understand what it means to forgive. The ego's definition of forgiveness is so implanted in my mind that I have to continually remind myself of its true meaning. The world I see is simply thoughts projected outward. The thoughts I project are not true thoughts. They are not the thoughts I think with God, and so they do not really create; what I see is not real. There is, therefore, nothing to forgive.

Additionally, what I do see is there because I called it into form. It is there because I want it there. There are no exceptions to this, though I often want to argue that there are. If the world exists as I have ordered it, then no one has done anything to me. There is nothing to forgive in the traditional sense. I see forgiveness as the understanding that no one and no thing has done anything to me. All happens according to my will, and all will be undone according to my will.

As I forgive these unreal thoughts, the sense of being vulnerable and weak dissolves from my mind, and I experience the power of God. So forgiveness is really just letting go of the mistaken thought and embracing the true thought. When I think the world has hurt me, I soon recognize that there is no world and that nothing was done to me. Forgiveness also recognizes that there is only One. There is only God, and in this perfect Wholeness, who is there to forgive? This is forgiveness.

Here is an example of how this played out in my mind. I called my brother twice, and both times he ignored my call. I knew he was available, because he was talking to business associates. I felt upset that he didn't answer my call. The situation called for forgiveness. First, I asked the Holy Spirit to look at it with me. Together we looked at the depth of my feeling. I felt betrayed and abandoned. I felt fearful as I wondered what I had done to offend him, and I thought of things that he might be angry about. I felt helpless to do anything about it and to restore balance to my life. I felt angry that he had made me feel like this.

Holy Spirit: Thank you for choosing to bring this to the light. These unforgiving thoughts were blocking the light that you are. Can you see that it was not his failure to call that blocked your light, but rather your thoughts about him not calling that upset you and left you in darkness?

It is useless to attempt controlling and changing anything in the world, because there is no world. Don't waste your time trying to get your brother to return your calls. Change the cause of the world you see, and you have indeed affected a real change and one that will bring you peace and joy. The salvation of the entire world is in your grasp through simple forgiveness, because the world is in your mind, as are the thoughts that created the world.

When your call was not returned, you saw that as an attack. Forgive that thought. You felt upset and angry with your brother. Forgive that thought. You felt unworthy, because he seemed not to find you important enough to return a call. Forgive that thought. You implied a need for your brother to change in order for you to feel good. Forgive that thought.

Perhaps you see a pattern here. Your brother did not call. That is what happened. Everything else that happened from that moment on was a result of misperceptions in your mind, which are easily corrected through forgiveness. Forgiveness will see that nothing happened, and peace will be restored to the mind. Your brother is perfectly innocent, and so are you. That is the only truth.

Me: I see how all the threat I perceived in the situation was just a result of my thoughts about it. I also see that I am not really forgiving him, but rather forgiving the projections I put on him. It feels pretty silly now that I made up all these stories about him, and I have no idea what was really happening. I could think of lots of perfectly innocent stories that would explain his actions, but I choose simply to forgive the need to know those stories or to have any of them be true. I accept that the only truth is that we are both innocent, and nothing that appears to be happening is relevant. Nothing that seems to be happening can change the nature of our innocence.

Lesson 63

The light of the world brings peace to every mind through my forgiveness.

Jesus tells me that I am the light of the world; then he tells me that my function as the light is to forgive. Now he tells me that I bring peace to every mind through my forgiveness. It is not through words that I forgive, but through the correction of my beliefs. It is all done at the level of the mind, and because there is only one mind, every time I forgive, it is done for the entire Sonship. Each seeming part will accept the peace of forgiveness when they are ready, but as I forgive, I become a symbol of forgiveness.

Whatever we choose to believe, that belief is spread throughout the Sonship. So if I choose anger, I am spreading anger throughout the Sonship. If I choose forgiveness, I am spreading forgiveness throughout the Sonship. Seeing it in this way makes my responsibility very clear to me. I am always affecting the entire Sonship with each thought that I believe and accept as true.

This morning, as I was doing this lesson, a thought about something that happened last night came to mind. When my mind seems to be wandering, I gently return my attention to the lesson, but first I notice the thoughts to see if they relate to the lesson. Sometimes it is through these thoughts that the Holy Spirit shows me something about the lesson. In this case I was being reminded that I had judged someone, and so I went over the incident with Holy Spirit and allowed Him to correct my thinking.

It doesn't matter if I do the forgiveness in the moment, or if I do it at another time. Time and space are no more real than anything else in the illusion. I can forgive just as fully something that happened when I was a child as I can forgive something that is happening in the moment. Another thing I was reminded of is that I am not forgiving that person for anything she did; I am forgiving my perception of the person. Again, it is all done at the level of mind. I am forgiving not behavior, but thoughts.

Holy Spirit: Myron, you have made a habit of answering each grievance with the thought that there is another way to see this. This opens your mind to My correction. In doing this, you are lighting the world with your forgiveness. Your mind is the source of the world, and so you are lighting your mind. Your mind is one with all other aspects of the Son, and so you light the mind for all. Do not be concerned that others may not be ready to open their eyes to the light. Because one shuts out the light does not mean the light is not there. When they are ready, the light your forgiveness provides will be waiting for them.

Lesson 64

Let me not forget my function.

Jesus says that this is just another way of saying: "Let me not wander into temptation." The temptation is to believe that there is meaning in anything that I see in the world, and that I should therefore base my decisions on what I am experiencing. Of course, I must do things in the world, but at the same time, I know that what I do does not matter. It is only choosing which teacher I am listening to when I do these things that has any meaning for me. As I choose the Holy Spirit as my teacher, I remember my function.

My function is to forgive. I can only be happy as I fulfill my function. I can do this, because it is the function given me by God, and He would not give His beloved child a function he could not fill. Every choice I make is a choice for happiness or for unhappiness, a choice to attack or a choice to love and forgive. Regardless of how complicated the ego would make the situation seem, those are the only two choices I have.

I ask the Holy Spirit what to do in specific situations. I ask Him what would be the most helpful thing for me to say to a person. I ask for guidance frequently. I set my intent this morning to be the servant of Love, rather than to be the director of the day.

At the San Francisco conference, I was discussing the Course with my friend, Larry. I said something to him, and he mentioned that he did not see it exactly that way. I was so surprised (the ego always thinks it has the answers) that I began to argue my point. Fairly quickly I noticed this error and stopped. I watched my mind as I did so and noticed how hard it is for the ego to let go of the desire to be right. Slowly, the ego need to convince Larry of its position began to dissolve away, as I remembered my function and forgave the situation.

The ego thinks its function is to understand everything and to convince everyone else to join its point of view. I am not the ego, and this is not my function as the Son of God. My only function is the one God gave me. I am to forgive in every circumstance. This is the way I extend Love, and this is the way I save the world. I can do this. It is really very easy. Just as I did in this case, I choose love rather than choosing to be right.

I also noticed that needing to be right was another way of holding on to the ego-identity. By making my view of the Course important, I am saying that I am one who believes this way; I am that belief. This is an ego-identity. This is the way the ego is formed; one belief layered over another. When I identify with these beliefs I am saying that this is what I am. In relinquishing the need to convince Larry of this viewpoint, I was also relinquishing the idea that I am that ego-identity; I am not that. I am that I Am, which is an identity without the limits imposed by beliefs.

For just a moment that evening, I identified with my ego, because I forgot my function. I forgot to step back before I spoke and to allow Spirit to speak through me. Mary Gerard (author of *Visions*) said something in her class at the conference that is helping me to remember to do this. She said (and demonstrated through action), "Step back, step aside, and invite the Holy Spirit to lead." That is a very helpful visual for me and a dance that I am willing to do all through the day.

Holy Spirit: One day you will not need to ask for any specific guidance, because you will hear only My Voice. You will reach this point by asking Me for guidance now. You are doing exactly what you need to do. You know you are following My guidance by the way you feel. Do you feel joyful and peaceful? If not, then look with Me at the thoughts which are blocking these feelings. This is all you need to do. When it seems more complex than this, it is because you are listening to the ego, rather than to Me.

Me: Sometimes I think I am doing well, and sometimes I think I am just kidding myself. I begin to wonder, "What if I am totally wrong?" I forget that it is simple and that if I am in peace, I am listening to the Voice of Truth. Thank You for the reminder.

Lesson 65

My only function is the one God gave me.

I think I have many functions. I think that it is my function to be a mom, to earn a living, to do good works, to be a minister and a writer and a counselor. None of these is my function. What I do with the body will never be my function; they are just things I do. They are useful only when I am mindful of my true function, as I do them. What I do helps me to learn my true function, if that is my choice. My true function is to remember who I am, that is to stop believing I am an individual and to stop believing my salvation lies in blaming someone else for all that seems to be wrong with me.

Holy Spirit, I have been feeling a little overwhelmed with all the things there are for me to do lately. I don't know what to do with this feeling, but I suspect that it has something to do with misunderstanding my function. Could You please talk to me about that?

Holy Spirit: It is not about what you are doing or not doing. The unease is about what you are telling yourself about it. When you place value on what you do, you will suffer when your doing does not meet your expectations. You have one function, and that is to forgive your thoughts. That is all that you need to do. Everything else that you do can be used to prompt the forgiveness, but that is its only value. Withdraw the misplaced value, and your expectations will fall away, and with your expectations, your anxiety will fall away as well.

An example of this would be these lessons. Your journaling is for your own healing, and if you make this process about getting the message out, you will be making your own function in place of the function God gave you. Your function is your own healing, and in that healing you will be a model for someone else.

If you make being a model for someone else your function, you will be listening to the ego, instead of the Voice for God. You will experience yourself as ego and feel anxious and guilty. Do not stop what you are doing, but always ask yourself, "Why am I doing this?" The question you want to ask about everything is, "What is this for?" If the answer is anything other than remembering who you are, then you are listening to the wrong voice.

Me: Thank You for helping me with this. I am going to watch my thoughts today and notice when I am trying to bring the ego into our work together. I am willing to see this differently.

2011

For several years I have been looking at my thoughts for the purpose of allowing the Holy Spirit to heal my mind. As time went on, I began to realize that most of my thoughts were untrue. Now I realize that thinking is the process of separation. It is always about separating, sorting, comparing, judging and decision-making, all things I used to think were important and valuable skills.

What I am coming to understand is that getting more proficient at thinking is just getting more proficient at being an ego. This is the reason I am learning to let go of thinking. I am learning to allow the mind to become a tool for true communication, rather than a playground for ego. As I free my mind from ego thinking, the thoughts I think with God become the only thing in my mind.

It is still helpful for me to notice the thoughts I believe. Behind each thought is the belief that sourced it. It is this belief that I ask the Holy Spirit to heal. So as long as I am aware of thoughts in my mind, I will use them to help us wake up. However, the mind can be very busy with thoughts, "monkey chatter"; the ego doesn't care what is going on in the mind so long as it is something, anything to keep me away from Silence. I am practicing letting this go. Here is a passage from *The Teachings of the Inner Ramana* that is helpful to me: "When the mind chatters, it chatters because you are listening to it." It is very helpful for me to step away from that.

And so I remain vigilant. My feelings tell me that I am entertaining an untrue thought that indicates a false belief in my mind. I ask the Holy Spirit for correction, and in spite of heavy resistance, I continue the process of learning to give up thinking, which will open my mind to knowing. The value I have found in maintaining the vigilance and doing the work necessary to achieve a think-free zone in my mind is peace! Freedom! Joy! Think I'll stick it out and go for the gold: awakening to my Self!

Grievances Obscure the Truth in My Mind

Lesson 66

My happiness and my function are one.

Jesus is going to a lot of trouble here to be sure that I understand that accepting my function is going to make me happy. He needs to do this, because I have always been taught that God wants sacrifice. Jesus says that this is not true. Also, I have always believed that my happiness usually entailed someone's loss. Jesus says that this is not true either. It is pretty simple, really. God gave me my function. God wants only my happiness. My function, which is forgiveness, must therefore make me happy.

I was thinking about work and how competitive sales are. I have noticed a difference in the way I feel when I get a customer from a competitor. For a long time, I would be elated if I won a customer from someone else. I thought that this was happiness. But it isn't the kind of happiness Jesus is talking about. If someone has to lose for me to be happy, then I have not won.

First, it is reinforcing my belief that we are separate, and that is not a happy result. Also, it is the kind of pleasure that is very short-lived. If I take from someone, I believe I have attacked and can only expect attack in return. This is not a happy thought either. But this is my job, and if I don't pick up customers, soon I won't have that job. I wonder how I am supposed to see this.

Holy Spirit: Do you remember yesterday's lesson, Myron? It is not about what you are doing or not doing. The question is what are you using it for? Are you using your job to increase your stature by being a better salesperson and by winning more customers? Are you seeing your position and your status in your company as who you are? Are you making getting more customers your goal in life, your purpose, and is your happiness dependent on that success?

It is possible to do the same job without making the doing of it your goal. You are kind and thoughtful to the people you visit. You accord the same respect to the people who can never benefit you as you do the ones who buy from you. You sincerely care about the people you meet on the job. You lift them up with words and thoughts.

You are peaceful and joyful when you visit, and they are drawn to that and want it for themselves. You don't have a lot of customers because you are a great salesperson. You have customers because you are remembering your true function. In this way everyone wins, as you have opportunity after opportunity to choose the Voice for God, and they are given opportunities to see what that looks like and to make the same choice for themselves.

Me: Please help me to remain mindful of my true purpose all day. Seeing my work in this way creates in me a sense of excitement and joy while doing the work. I was beginning to lose interest in work, thinking that I should be doing more with my ministry. It is good to be reminded that my ministry is wherever I am.

2009

I wrote the above and received Holy Spirit's answer in 2007. Yesterday I was visiting a customer who used to buy from another company. I remembered how competitive I felt at the time. I thought about the excitement of winning, and I realized that I did not win at all. I did not understand what winning was. At one time, the way I did business was more akin to war. I saw what I wanted, planned my strategy, and attacked. When I seemed to win I felt elated, but only briefly, because winning comes with its opposite: losing. Attack brings fear of being attacked. Winning a customer creates the fear of losing a customer.

As I spoke to that customer, I thought of the competitor who used to sell to them. I remembered the resentment and anger I used to feel when I thought of this company. I remembered the fear when I saw them talking to my customer. I can hardly believe I felt such animosity toward these people, these children of God. How could I have ever thought that it was my function to cause harm to someone, and how could I have ever thought it would make me happy to do so? Holy Spirit, thank You for the clarity I have received from You over the years. Please continue to help me remember my true function.

2011

My prayer now, when I go see a potential customer, is not that I should make a sale, but that I might be truly helpful to this person. I surrender myself to the Holy Spirit in this case, as I do in any other, when I ask, "What would you have me do? What would you have me say? How would you have me respond? Please make me a blessing to this person." My job is so much more peaceful and joyful than it used to be. When I think back and realize the stress I inflicted on myself when I thought my job was about winning, taking, and seeing others as guilty and myself as victim, I am amazed that I could tolerate it as long as I did. I am truly grateful for the healing of my mind.

Lesson 67

Love created me like itself.

2007

I can only get to God's definition of me by looking honestly at all that I think I am and being willing to see it differently. This is an idea I repeat over and over in every lesson, because it is the key to my salvation. It is good to remind myself frequently of what it is that I am in truth, but it is necessary to see clearly what I have substituted for God's creation in order to allow my error to be corrected.

I look at the idea that I am special and important and needed, and that seems so good. It feels good. I like it. This thought, of course, does not look at the other side of the coin, and with the ego there is always an opposite. My specialness precludes my wholeness. It is lonely, because it means I must be separate.

I am important to some people, but they sometimes change their minds, and there are about seven billion people who don't know I exist and who would never miss me if I died tomorrow. How important could I be? I comfort myself with the thought that, if only one person needs me, that is enough, but I know that this person would continue to exist without me and do just fine. Does that person really need me? Am I really important to even that one person?

What I have made is not a good thing. But I can see it differently, if I am willing to give up the meaning I have substituted for truth. And so I remind myself frequently that there is another way to see myself. I was created like God, and am still like God. Thoughts do not leave their source and so the memory of my true Self is still in my mind, where it was placed by God in my creation. I can be aware of those thoughts, but I must first be willing to release the old idea of who I am.

It seems like a no-brainer, but it is really hard. I think that I am the ego/body that I call Myron. Now I am being told that Myron is not real and doesn't exist. This is very frightening to think about. Sure, there is something else, and it is really good, but I don't remember that experience, and the only way to remember it is to give up all I think I am. Talk about walking on water!

Holy Spirit: Myron, that you can confront even this much of the great lie is a huge step out of the ego belief system. Do not be concerned about your unwillingness to go further at this moment. This is a gradual, step-by-step process. You are not being asked to do more than you can do. We do not want you to step into fear. You have enough fear in your life right now. We want you to see that fear is not a necessary component of life. Be as patient with yourself as We are.

Allow yourself to become more comfortable with this idea. Think often of what you are moving toward: a life of ease and joy. Remind yourself frequently that you are very holy and very loved. I assure you that individuality is a poor substitute for wholeness. You are waking up to your glory, Myron, and that is what you want to remember as you go through your day. When fear and trepidation come up, invite Me to look at it with you. Do not be afraid to look. It is an illusion and cannot hurt you. Looking at it is the way you become free from it.

Me: I take great comfort in knowing that I am not alone and that there are others who have gone before me and will lead me out of my confusion. I thank you, Jesus, for being the first to do that.

2009

Recently, I have been taking this idea a little further, as I have been willing to give up more of the self-identity. Often during the day, or as often as I care to remember, I use a mantra. I have tried several but have settled on, "I am that I Am." This is the best definition of Self that I can find. I am something with no limits; I simply am. I breathe in on "I am" and out on "that I Am." I allow myself to accept the holiness of the statement to the extent that I am willing to do so.

I also pay attention to the limited ideas that I am identifying with. I think of myself as a writer and a teacher. But I am not that. A good writer and an effective teacher is a limit on who I am. It sounds good, but it is still not who I am. While I have been using this process to release some false ego identities, the ego has not gone down silently and gently.

The more I do this, the more frantic that part of the mind becomes. It absolutely does not want me to give up my identity as it is defined by ego. As I do, the ego becomes very vicious and sometimes I seem to be drowning in negative, fearful thoughts.

Holy Spirit, this is very weird to me. I hear the ego; I feel the impact of the ego-thoughts, but I don't succumb completely, as I once did. I don't sink into a fog of total forgetfulness, as I once did, but I am not oblivious to the fear, either. I need help to do this.

Holy Spirit: Yes, you do need help, my dear friend, and you receive help every step of the way. The Love of God upholds you, as you move more completely into this new process. Myron, it will help you to stop looking around and ahead. Do not look around to see how you compare to others on the path. This is the ego's way of distracting and discouraging you. It is also the ego's way of keeping you in separation thinking.

Do not look ahead at all that seems to lie before you. The seemingly endless road ahead is an optical illusion. Trust that the long road ahead will fold in upon itself, as you allow yourself to be carried down it. There is neither distance nor time, except in the ego-thinking mind, which is in itself an illusion. As you let go of the ego-self, time and distance unravels as well.

Me: 'Thank You' seems an inadequate reply, Holy Spirit. I am grateful for Your ever-present help.

2011

Reading my journaling of this lesson created in me an odd feeling. I see the slow progression, as I moved deeper into this lesson over a period of time. Evidently, I am ready to go even deeper, because the Holy Spirit has guided me to *The Teachings of the Inner Ramana,* which is devoted to letting the self go and to reaching the Self, and now I don't think my progression is as slow.

In the past I have been sporadic in my vigilance, as I let go of the ego. In just the three or so weeks I have been listening to the CDs and reading *The Teachings of the Inner Ramana,* my attention has not wavered. My mind has become quieter than it ever has been. I don't feel the kind of fear of loss of self that I have had in the past. The fear I do experience seems a bit removed, as if I am standing back from it and watching the experience of fear. I have had a couple of experiences of letting go of a concept completely and then laughing like a loon, the joy just bursting out of me.

How amazing!

But I am still not willing to go past my thoughts to the "awareness of a blazing light" in which I recognize myself as love. That felt disappointing to me, and I remembered that I am not that thought, nor the mind that thought it. I am that I Am. I am exactly as God created me. I forgive the idea that my seeming failure makes me a failure. God is not a failure, so I cannot be a failure either. A great deal of vigilance is still necessary.

Even though I have been letting go of the thinking mind for a while now, this new, deeper, more consistent effort is almost like starting over. Or maybe it's like I have gone from crawling to toddling along. Now I am learning to run; same effort, just different stages.

Lesson 68

Love holds no grievances.

If I hold a grievance against anyone, I am teaching myself that I am separate from God. In fact, that is the point of grievances; they defend against the idea that I am one with God. To be one with God would mean I cannot be Myron as an individual body/personality. Grievances are the opposite of God in every way. To have a grievance proves that there is more than one. To have a grievance proves that I am not wholeness and love. It keeps the ego system of separateness nicely in place and proves it exists. This is my hidden agenda when I hold a grievance.

I can look honestly at all my grievances and see that they are the cause of my misery and suffering. Doing this can be painful, because it requires that I look at the system of projection in which I tried to put outside myself what I couldn't stand to look at within myself. It requires that I withdraw those projections and bring them back into myself, so that I can allow them to be healed, and who wants to do that? But here is the thing: it is the only way that I can be healed and return to happiness. Since I have experienced this healing to some degree, I am motivated to continue it, even though it is still sometimes hard to do.

Here is an example of a way in which I used this lesson. I was sharing my personal view of some Course ideas with a friend who did not agree with me. I found myself feeling mildly annoyed (which Jesus tells us is just a veil thrown over intense rage), and then I felt guilty. (I know that this is an attack on her, even if I do not say anything to her.) I wanted to push this away and not think about my attitude, and I was tempted to do so, since I never actually said anything. Instead, I embraced these thoughts and allowed myself to fully explore this with Jesus, who tells us in the text that I must be very honest with myself, for "we must hide nothing from each other."

I thought that this woman just didn't get it. I thought that she was kidding herself, because she didn't want to see the truth. I thought that I was much further along and that this was why she didn't understand it as I did. I thought that she was really getting on my nerves. I thought that I didn't even want to be around her, and I wished she would go away. I wondered why on earth I cared that she didn't agree with me and why I felt so strongly about it.

I felt intensely guilty and ashamed of these thoughts. At the same time I realized that there was a much deeper meaning here, but my emotions were keeping me from seeing what it might be. As much as I hated seeing these petty thoughts in myself, I recognized that not looking at them is the way I protect and perpetuate them. I asked the Holy Spirit to show me another way to see this. I didn't think of anything in particular, but knew I was willing, because I don't want to think like this. I trust that my thoughts will be corrected, whether I receive anything obvious or not.

Me: Holy Spirit, could You help me to understand that episode better?

Holy Spirit: Yes. You have probably noticed that when you are in any way bothered because someone does not agree with you, you feel the need to correct them. Sometimes you notice the need, and sometimes it is just a feeling of general and unspecified discomfort. Often you realize that this is not an urge that comes from God, and so you do not act on it.

Sometimes, you have acted on it and have regretted it, so you learned to stop yourself. But usually you don't fully explore the underlying feelings and thoughts, so you don't realize how strong the feelings are and how unpleasant the thoughts become. It is very good that you allowed this to happen. You are not really giving Me a thought to correct, unless you look at that thought.

Behind your need to correct your friend was your need to be right. You forgot for a moment the purpose of doing this work, which is to heal your mind and to awaken to your true identity. In needing to be right, you gave it that purpose, instead. When this happens the Course becomes just another way to hide from God.

What you were fighting was not really your friend's views but your own split mind. Part of your mind wanted to be right and the other part knew that this was not your purpose. You did not want to see this, and so you projected the whole ugly thing onto your friend. Then she was the one who was wrong. She was to blame for your discomfort, and you wanted her quickly gone, so you could maintain the illusion of being "right".

Because you had formed the habit of seeing errors in your thinking and bringing them to Me for correction, you were not as strongly attached to your error as you once would have been. You were able to step back from it enough to ask for help. Don't worry about the "ugly" thoughts that brought you shame. Ego-thoughts will happen as long as the illusion of separation remains in place. Recognize that they are not the truth and do not identify with them.

Me: As I read this, I notice that this was also an opportunity to remember that when I cling to these thoughts, I am also reinforcing the ego-identity. By being willing to relinquish this identity as a separated self that has its own agenda that is different from her agenda, I am revealing more of my true Self.

I had a story going about being a better Course student and being right, and I was attached to and identified with that story. I was saying to myself that I was a person who was usually right about these things and superior to others. By looking at those thoughts without fear or judgment, I was able to realize that I am not that thought; it does not define me. It was an idea that I held in my mind briefly, and then let go. I am not that.

Holy Spirit: Yes, Myron. Do you notice that even without the thought of being right and being superior, you still exist? Since you still exist without that idea, you must be more than that idea. As you dismantle these little boxes you created to define yourself, you will re-discover the Self you have traded away for the experience of being separate.

Lesson 69

My grievances hide the light of the world in me.

Here I am, the light of the world, but who can see that light when it is obscured by all the grievances I hold? Even I have lost sight of the light I am created to be, and imagine myself as existing outside that light, somewhere on the other side of the grievances. That is the little self I made. It stands guard over my grievances and keeps them in place so that the little self will continue to exist. So now I need an exercise to help me return to my Self, even though I have never, in reality, left. What an absurd position I find myself in.

Jesus reminds me that I cannot fail in this because it is God's Will that I succeed. He reminds me that He is with me and that my part is to be willing and that He will do the rest. In fact, it is important that I lend only my willingness and not try to do more.

My focus today is going to be on the grievances that are keeping me in hell. There are many ways to be aware of the grievances. I need only look for guilt, sickness, attack thoughts, anger, fear, depression, anxiety. These seem like many different things, but they are really just different expressions of the same error. They are projections meant to shield me from God. As I become aware of each thought, I will imagine myself gently brushing away the cloud that is keeping me from the light.

Holy Spirit: Myron, please remember that this is a process. You are feeling uneasy, because you can think of so many grievances, and you think that, as soon as you release one, another pops up. Do not let this concern you. You are doing what you came to do. You are noticing and allowing. It is a temptation to judge the results and to find yourself wanting. That is just the ego thought-system trying to reassert itself. You no longer want to listen to that voice. Nor is it necessary that you catch every thought. Just work with those that you notice, and be willing not to exclude any purposely.

I know that sometimes you think you are not getting anywhere, but I assure you that you are making great progress. Perhaps it would be helpful if you were to make a list of all the positive changes in your life. I do not mean so much the material changes, but think about how much joy you have in your life now. When was the last time you have experienced depression? Remember how pervasive that was in your life just a few years ago? Joy is your nature as God's Son, and the fact that you are experiencing it more and more should show you how much closer you are to your goal. The difference, Myron, is that you are more often choosing salvation as your goal.

Me: Thank You for addressing my uncertainties. Indeed, yesterday I felt like I was losing ground. I felt rushed and listless. My mind felt like it was wrapped in a fog. I didn't have the clarity of purpose I have had in the last few days, and that disturbed me. But, when I think about it, I realize that I still noticed when I was listening to ego-thoughts and I still expressed my willingness to see differently. I was in a fog, but I wasn't lost in the fog. I am so grateful for that.

Lesson 70

My salvation comes from me.

My salvation does not lie in the world I think is outside me. There is no one out there to save me through a special relationship, no man or best friend who will complete me and bring happiness to my life, no doctor with medicine who will make me happy by curing what ails me. There is no job that will fulfill me. I am just wasting time looking from one idol to another for my joy. The answer is in my mind, and only in my mind, because that is where everything is.

I will continue my practice of noticing my thoughts and asking for correction. In this lesson, Jesus offers to hold my hand as I pass through the clouds of illusions. He is saying that I must pass through them. I cannot jump over them or go around them. I must look at them, but I don't have to do it alone, and, in fact, am not to do it alone. Jesus reinforces how important this is by making an unusual and strong statement. He says: *"If it helps you, think of Me holding your hand and leading you. AND I ASSURE YOU, IT WILL BE NO IDLE FANTASY."* Wow! I really am not alone in this, and I have powerful help.

Me: Holy Spirit, I have a favorite fantasy where everyone in my world thinks I am okay, and sometimes they think I am great. My mind is split on this issue. Part of my mind knows that seeking outside myself for happiness is a real waste of time. But another part of my mind wants to believe that there is still something out there that is worth having and will make me happy. I think this is why I have such a fear of exposing my thoughts. I want my secret sins to be kept a secret so that people will love me. Can You please help me to see this differently?

Holy Spirit: Thank you for asking for My help. You think that if everyone could be aware of your dark thoughts that they would be as appalled as you are. But think of this; you are not separated from your brother, and there is only one mind. It is not so much that you should not have separate thoughts, but that you cannot.

When you bring Me your thoughts, you are not doing it so that I can know what they are. We have no secrets from each other. You bring them to Me because YOU need to look at them and you need to release them. I know who you really are, and I simply disregard the ego-thoughts, because they are nothing. As together we look at these dark thoughts and release them, you will know only the truth about yourself. Some of your thoughts appear to be evil, simply because you have judged them so, but they are really nothing.

If you want to protect your thoughts from others a little while longer, then you may, but realize what you are deciding by doing so. You have said yourself that they are keeping you in hell. Why don't you begin by bringing Me your idea that you need to hide your thoughts. Together we will see the insubstantial nature of the fear that you are evil, because you hold ego-thoughts. You want to believe that your delusional thoughts, no matter how evil, have left you unstained by their darkness. The way to prove this is to expose them to the light and to see that you are not condemned, but shining with your innocence.

Another thought:

I have been working diligently on letting go of the idea that I can think my way out of the illusion. I notice my thoughts, and then I ask myself who is thinking this? Who is the "I" that I refer to? I remind myself that I am not that I. As I let go of the ego-identities, I see the truth of who I am more clearly. I let go of thinking on my own, and the thoughts of God flood my mind. Well, maybe flood is too strong a word; they are trickling in right now, but I see a flood coming.

As I was doing this recently, I became discouraged because it suddenly felt very hard. I temporarily lost my clarity of purpose; I thought about the apparent impossibility of giving up the idea that I can have my own private thoughts. I can give up making decisions on my own, and I can give up judging things. Then I read something Regina wrote from her Inner Teacher; it appeared to me with perfect timing, just the words I needed to hear. It was as if He were writing just for me through Regina. Once again, I am deeply touched and amazed at the perfection of Jesus' plan for salvation.

Here is what I read:

> If you look at the idea "This will be difficult" you will see it as only an idea. If you hold up the idea and shout that it is true, you are attached to the idea because you are holding to it. But if you let go of the idea, it will go away. The idea has no life, and so it can have no attachments. This idea is not attached to you; you are attached to it. If you let it go, it will go, because an idea cannot have a desire of its own that will cause it to stay.
>
> It is true that if you are not finished with this idea, it will return to you. But if you can let it go once, you can let it go again. And in any moment that you are not holding to the idea, you can make the decision immediately to put aside the "I" thought, go into your Heart, and join with Me.

Salvation Is Letting Go of Grievances

Lesson 71

Only God's plan for salvation will work.

2007

This lesson tells me that God's plan will work and that no other plan will work. The conflict I suffer is because I want God's plan, but I don't want to give up my plan. I am trying to do both, and because they are diametrically opposed, it won't work. My plan is to make everyone and everything outside myself responsible for my salvation and that which I can blame for my unhappiness. God's plan is that I forgive all these grievances. Trying to do both only leaves me confused and depressed. The answer is to choose God's plan, or in other words, to listen only to His Voice.

It seems like this would be easy. God has the answer, and I want the answer. What could be easier? But the ego plan calls to me, and I have formed lifetime habits of listening to that call. I have learned to identify with the ego, and so it feels like releasing the ego will be the end of who I am. I see my resistance in so many little ways, and so I will use those symbols of resistance to change my mind. As always, I will bring them to the light and allow the Holy Spirit to shine the darkness away.

Holy Spirit: This is truly an "all or none" Course, and that is the good news. It is the uncertainty and the vacillation that has in the past kept you in hell. Finally, here is a straight and narrow path. That you have found this path and are walking it means you are ready for it. You will stray from this path, but do not be discouraged by this temporary lapse.

There is only one plan that works and only one Voice that answers your call. Though you will hear another voice, you know that that voice is not for you. Let it call out, but do not believe it; it is a senseless call and will not take you where you want to go. If you turn your ear from the foolishness of the ego, you will hear the joyful song of the Voice for God. Follow that sound and only that sound. The ego does not know the way home; the Voice for God does.

Me: I want to go home, Holy Spirit. I want to go home more than I want to play in the illusion. Please remind me when I become tempted to lose myself in some ego-story going on around me. It is such a sad little offering, these ego-dramas. Why do I fall prey to them so often? I don't want this any more. I cannot be made to believe ego-thoughts. This is a choice I made, and now I change my mind.

Holy Spirit: Let us look together at this statement of desire, Myron. Look boldly and do not be afraid of what you see.

Me: In the past I have safely assigned the completion of this task to the future. Yes, I work on it every day, but in my mind I have thought of it as something that is very difficult and takes a long time. I have thought that in some lifetime down the road I will wake up and remember my true nature. But now I realize that this is not hard. All that keeps me from awakening is a thought, an ego-identity thought. I reject thoughts, and change my mind every day. It is not hard to do.

All that I am really doing now with these daily practices is convincing myself that I want to wake up. When that is done, I relinquish all value I have placed in seeing myself as a separate individual, and my mind is changed. I am awake. I will stop telling myself this is hard and will take a long time. Instead, I will face my fears of dying to the ego and allow the Holy Spirit to correct my thinking about this.

The thought of one "eye-blink away" enters my mind. I will wake in the blink of an eye. I wonder what that would be like, and the ego starts weaving stories around it, stories that quickly turn frightening. I reject this line of thought, because it merely brings me deeper into the thinking mind, which is the ego, and this is the opposite direction from where I want to be. The ego cannot imagine wakefulness, and so I will not use the thinking mind to do this.

Holy Spirit, thank You for helping me to see my resistance and my fear. I am willing to look with you on all the dark and fearful places in my mind and to have these healed. In spite of the fear that this thought engenders, I still want to do it. I feel the fear, but I don't believe it.

2011

I no longer need convincing that God's plan is the only one that works and that I want His plan and only His plan. Now I simply practice. I watch my mind and notice when I have fallen back into the habit of looking for salvation outside myself. This is the same as holding a grievance, because if I want something to be different, I am holding a grievance against what is.

I am learning to surrender completely to the guidance of the Holy Spirit. I am learning to ask those questions frequently. What would You have me do, now? Where would You have me go? What would You have me say? It is not asking the question that assures the answer. It is wanting that answer more than I want my own answer that opens my mind to His Voice.

There is still resistance. This morning, as I started my lesson, my mind kept wandering. Finally, I stopped a moment and paid attention to what I was thinking. I noticed that I was feeling anxiety because I think I need to get some bookkeeping done, and I need to write more for my book, something that I have not been able to do lately. I just had to laugh. My salvation does not lie in these things. I will not make plans on my own. I surrender this to Your perfect plan, Holy Spirit, and wait for Your prompt.

Sometimes the ego baits the hook with something I find harder to resist. Yesterday was an example. I used to think that this was hard, if not impossible. I used to think that I couldn't do it, or if I could, it would take lifetimes. I used to be afraid that I was completely wrong. There is still an attraction in my mind to these thoughts, and the ego brought them out as an enticement.

It was harder for me to turn away from these thoughts, but though it took longer and felt harder, the process was the same.

Through daily practice, I am learning not to give my attention or my belief to the ego-thinking mind. I am doing this through vigilance, noticing when it is happening and then surrendering my mind and my action to One Who knows God's plan for my salvation.

Lesson 72

Holding grievances is an attack on God's plan for salvation.

Jesus is getting more specific. Not only are my grievances holding me back, but they are literally an attack on God. As I hold something against another person, I am holding it against God. I am actively fighting God's plan for my salvation and putting my own plan (defensiveness) in its place. I may not know much, but I know that my plan is not working. And it doesn't take any kind of special discernment to realize that, as I attack God, the unconscious guilt is building up.

This lesson centers on our desire to be a body and to make others a body, including God. If I see myself as a body, then I must see God as a body as well, because I cannot possibly see my creator as different from myself. I am very clear that seeing myself as a body is an attack on myself. I went from being whole, complete, and perfect in every way, to being vulnerable, weak, fragile, guilty, fearful, dying and separate, especially separate. If that is not an attack, I don't know what is.

Then I made God into a body as well. So I have created God in the image of what I think I am, and so have attacked His Divinity as well as my own. No wonder I am so full of guilt and fear. No wonder I made an entire world on which to project my guilt.

I ate breakfast in a restaurant at the hotel where I was staying.

It took an extraordinary amount of time to get very bad food, and I became impatient and angry. My server had to be the worst waitress I have ever had, and I really began to resent her. I noted that I had relegated her to body. Her body was slow. It was what she did that annoyed me, and doing is a body function. And her body is hers and mine is mine, so we are separate. I even remember thinking that, if I acted that way to my customers, I wouldn't have many customers and couldn't afford to eat here. Oh yes, we are definitely different, I assured myself.

I reminded myself that this is an attack on God, since I am separating and making different what is whole and the same. I started noticing other separation thoughts, and with each one gave myself the same reminder: this is an attack on God. Then I remembered this from the end of the text of *A Course in Miracles*: *"Choose once again, if you would take your place among the saviors of the world, or would remain in hell, and hold your brothers there."*

I was filled with such gratitude for my brothers who seemed to be offering me reason to condemn them but are really offering me this precious opportunity to choose again. When my waitress came by my table, I asked her if she was working the whole room alone, and she said that she was and that this was her first night to work. She apologized for the delays, and I assured her that it didn't matter, and believe me, I was not just saying it. I left her a very excessive tip, not because she gave me great service, but in thanksgiving for her true gift to me, the opportunity to lay my grievance down and to choose love instead.

Me: Holy Spirit, what is salvation? I do not know.

Holy Spirit: Precious child, salvation is being saved from the error in your mind that sees you as a body. How could this be? How could the Son of God be trapped in this illusion of a little bit of flesh and bones, born to suffer and then to die? How could this be? Salvation is knowing that this cannot be. You are not this body, you do not suffer, and you will never die. This is salvation.

Look with Me, you holy child of God, at each bit of seeming proof that you are less than whole and complete. Do not be afraid to look at the grievances and attacks that seem to be your only defense, and do not be afraid to lay them down. The love of God will sustain you, as nothing you have ever devised could do. Has a lifetime of anger protected you from your demons? It has not, nor will it ever. But you are not alone, and there is a plan for your salvation.

It is not a plan that pleases the ego, and be glad of that. The ego argues that it is unimpressive and boring, and yet you have seen that bringing your grievances into the light and allowing Me to correct your erroneous thoughts has brought more joy into your life than you have ever before experienced. Your plans have not worked, and this plan has.

If one grievance seems bigger, scarier, or harder, it is only because you have seen some need to hold on to it and are reluctant to let it go. In truth there are no levels of error. An error is simply an error. The ego would have you try to figure out these problems and psychoanalyze them. It will use circular reasoning to keep you in the problem, rather than to solve it. The ego is self-serving and cares nothing for your salvation, and, in fact, actively fights against your salvation. When you accept your rightful place within God, where then is the ego? It will simply cease to exist. And that is salvation.

Lesson 73

I will there be light.

Again, Jesus is talking about the end of the idea that grievances are salvation, but now He is telling us that our part is to will this for ourselves. He says that the Holy Spirit cannot correct our thinking without our consent. He is reminding us that our wish-fulfillment matters in this world, but in truth it does nothing. Our will, combined with the Will of God, however, is powerful. If we apply our will to salvation, then it will be ours. Jesus reminds us again and again that we really do want happiness, rather than to be right about the illusion.

What really stood out to me is the line, "Your will is lost to you in this strange bartering, in which guilt is traded back and forth, and grievances increase with each exchange." I think that this is meaningful to me because I can see it so clearly in life. I make someone guilty, they in turn offer me guilt, and I accept it but then feel angry and resentful, even if I think they are right. This is what Jesus is asking me to give up, and in exchange I can have Heaven. So what am I waiting for?

I am remembering an encounter with a store clerk the other day. I stood before her with my gum and my money, and she continued her conversation with her friend, as if I were not there. I felt impatient. I thought that she should get a different job that did not require any level of customer service. I felt angry way out of proportion to the inconvenience. When I looked at this store clerk, I did not see her. I saw only my grievance against her. It was as if she were standing behind a mirror that reflected back to me what was in my mind.

As I took this moment in time to the Holy Spirit and asked that He enlighten me, I felt the desire to forgive myself the projections I had placed on her. I forgave the impatience within my mind. I forgave the thoughtlessness and self-centeredness that resided in my mind. I began to see that the Holy Spirit was showing me that, as I forgive and release those beliefs within myself, they will not be reflected back to me. The clerk may continue to do whatever she does, but what she does will not appear to me as personal attacks, and I will not return attack or in any way defend myself.

In the world it may not look like anything has changed. I may still stand before the clerk with my gum and my money. She may still continue her conversation with her friend and ignore me. I may still wait for her attention. But in truth, everything has now changed. Instead of seeing a guilty clerk, I see Christ in all Her innocence. From my healed mind, I see only healed brothers and sisters. What could there be to defend against?

I have been mind-watching closely these days, looking for opportunities to spot the guilt exchanges and the grievances. Every time I become aware of this happening, I remind myself that I just attacked God and that I am keeping myself in hell. I notice that I still believe I am protecting myself when I make someone else guilty. I am willing to give up that idea and am doing so each time I see it in action and choose differently.

Holy Spirit: Each grievance that you bring to Me for correction allows more light to shine forth as a beacon for others to follow. You save yourself, and in the process you save the Sonship. What else could you do with your time that so rivals your salvation in significance? To choose guilt is to choose hell. You have chosen guilt and grievances in the past, and it has not brought you safety or happiness. Choose differently now. Choose God by choosing to hear only His Voice.

Me: I choose to hear Your Voice. I will do this each time I am aware of an attack thought. That is my will.

Lesson 74

There is no will but God's.

I think I have a will different from God's. This is obvious, because here I am exercising that will in the form of this illusion. But I don't have to stay with this. I can realize that I was mistaken when I decided that I have a will different from God's, because in truth, that is not possible. There is only God's Will.

If there is only God's Will, there can be no conflict, because there is nothing to conflict with. So when I notice conflict in my life, I bring that conflict to the Holy Spirit and allow Him to show me the truth. He helps me to see how meaningless conflict is in the light of One Will.

I have been working with the idea of secrets and private

thoughts. I find that, although I want to have no private thoughts, there are some thoughts which I am not willing to share. I am in conflict. It is the Will of God that we are One. There can be no private thoughts in One, because who would I be keeping my thoughts from? So, in order for me to keep my secrets, I must keep myself separate, and this requires that I exercise a will which I believe is different from God's Will.

Really, there are no such things as private thoughts. There is only one mind, and so all thoughts are known by all. The illusion that I can keep certain thoughts to myself is a shared delusion. It is a shared conspiracy to pretend, as if I know only my own separate thoughts and cannot know yours. It is part of the ego plan to keep separation in place.

I notice many little conflicts all through the day as I make judgments. I am not happy with the circumstance in which I find myself, or I don't feel like someone likes me, and am uncomfortable with that. I get a phone call from someone I don't want to talk to. I'm feeling frustrated because the electrician has never shown up to finish the dab of work on my house that is still left undone. There are many conflicts that don't seem like a big deal, but, if I am in conflict, I have forgotten who I am, and it doesn't matter how big or small I think they are. I can have conflict or I can have peace, but I can't have both.

Holy Spirit: It is good that you are aware of conflict. It seems to you as if you have an endless number of conflicts that you must deal with and that it is going to be nearly impossible to get through them all. But there is really only one problem, and that is the idea of separation. You are not resolving conflicts, but rather using each conflict to remember that there is no separation. Each time you notice a conflict, rejoice that you have another opportunity to practice forgiveness.

Thank you, Holy Spirit. That is a more joyful outlook. I guess it is silly to be working on conflicts and then to feel conflicted about how that work is going.

2009

As I was reading this lesson this morning, the thought that really held me was that I am an expression of the Will of God. The ego is squirming as I surrender to and embrace that thought. It wants to claim ownership of self and tells me that I should be afraid of losing myself to God. I am an expression of the Will of God. I hear the ego, but I don't think I believe it any more. When I think of myself as an expression of the Will of God, I feel joy, even as I hear the ego urging me to run for my life. Holy Spirit, there is still some part of the mind that wants to believe the ego and to run from this joy. I give You that part. Please heal it.

2011

I was surprised this morning, as I did the lesson, to discover that this lesson still brings up fear of losing my will and being absorbed by another, alien will. It is this line that triggered my reaction:

"As an expression of the Will of God, you have no goal but His."

So I sat with this for a few moments. I noticed that I had just as much fear when I thought that I might never get past this resistance. Thinking about falling back into ego and losing the peace and joy I am experiencing as I am letting go of ego thinking is very depressing. So I visualized my favorite prayer. I placed this belief on the altar of light and asked the Holy Spirit to heal my mind. As I did this, I remembered to question who it is that wants to cling to the belief that there could be a will that is not God. It could only be the ego. I am not that. I am that I Am.

I began to remember that there is only God, and so only the Will of God exists. As a part of God, I am a part of that Will. I am only playing with the idea of a separate existence apart from all that is, and it is an idea that can never become real, no matter how absorbed I am in the play. There cannot be anything outside of all there is.

Whew! I felt like a child who momentarily believed that there was a monster under her bed, then was reminded that it was she who made up the monster. I feel relief and a return of peace. But if there is still doubt, Holy Spirit, I am open to looking at it and allowing all uncertainty to be healed.

Lesson 75

The light has come

Ken Wapnick calls this lesson a pep talk and reminds us not to feel guilty if we don't spend the day in joy and peace. If Jesus really expected us to get this today, why did he give us all those other lessons? On the other hand, David Hoffmeister said that he did each lesson as if this were the one that would wake him up. But no matter how I use them, lessons like this one are very encouraging, and I am excited to think what it will mean to me when I do make that final decision.

The light is here and always has been here, but as I am beginning to remove some of the blocks to this light, it is becoming visible to me. I am learning to see the world differently. I also know for certain that the darkness is just an idea and will be undone with any single unequivocal thought of wholeness. So far my thoughts of wholeness have not been pure. So I continue to do my practices, acknowledging the errors in my mind and asking for healing. I walk forward in trust.

One Problem, One Solution

Lesson 76

I am under no laws but God's.

2007

I remember when I first read this lesson; my immediate thought was that I would never have to diet again. Like many people, I started doing the Course because I wanted to make a better illusion, and so my understanding of it always centered on that desire. In this case, the lesson begins by very clearly stating:

> *You are not bound by them. Yet to understand that this is so, you must first realize salvation lies not there. While you would seek for it in things that have no meaning, you bind yourself to laws that make no sense.*

Salvation does not lie in making a better body, but rather in changing the purpose I give the body. The body's use is to prove separation and to keep it in place. I seem to be this separate individual, different from all other individuals. That is its purpose, and the laws I set up for it all guarantee that purpose will be met. Through this lesson, I am being reminded that I am not victim to these laws, but the maker of these laws. I decided on them.

To be free of the laws I made to govern the body, I must see another purpose for the body. I can see the body as a way out of specialness. But do I want to give up choices and who I am as Myron and the pleasures of the body? Well, I took assessment this morning, and I still have my ego-self firmly in place, so I guess the answer is no.

On the other hand, I am beginning to see the light. I am no longer so enthralled with the idea of individuality and of the body. I am becoming willing to see differently. As I begin to use the body to help me learn the lessons that Jesus has for me, I am changing the purpose of the body. Instead of using the body to prove separation and guilt, I am learning to use the body to change my mind.

Ken Wapnick really helped me to see this more clearly in *Journey through the Workbook*. He pointed out how I use the body to solve my problems. For instance, the problem is that I feel I am alone in the universe, because I think I destroyed God. The ego agrees that I am lonely and then invents special relationships and teaches me the laws of manipulation and seduction to keep a body near me. Ken goes on to explain how the ego uses the body to solve all problems, but I can see that it never really works. It is, after all, the prime directive of the ego to seek but not to find.

The ego solution cannot work because it is based on a false premise. The ego says that I am a victim of the world and of the body, my body and the body of others. But the bodies are all just reflections of a thought in my mind. THERE IS NOTHING OUT THERE. Everything I think I see with the body's eyes exists only in the mind. I have resisted this, because I have thought that I needed and wanted this separation story to continue. The world and this body are where I have hidden from God and from my guilt. I am beginning to remember that God loves me very much, and I am innocent.

Yes, I have made a lot of ridiculous laws, but remembering that the laws I made do not really supersede the laws of God is helping me to change my mind. I can believe I am living under the ego's laws, but I cannot make that the truth. I am under no laws but God's.

Me: Holy Spirit, I want to understand how this lesson applies to eating and the body, particularly to dieting.

Holy Spirit: If you believe you need to diet to control your weight, then you need to diet. If you believe you are a body, you need to eat, and you need to follow whatever laws of eating you believe will keep you healthy. Do not allow guilt to enter into this. Do not feel guilty because you believe you are a body. That is not helpful to you. Just notice the purpose you are giving the body and allow Me to help you see it differently.

For instance, why do you want to diet? What is the purpose of maintaining a certain size? Do you think that your happiness lies in keeping the body at a certain weight? And does that mean a different weight will make you unhappy? [Obviously I do.] *In this case you are using the body to solve a problem that is in the mind. Can you see this ever working?* [No, of course I cannot, and it never has.] *So you are using the body for the purpose of proving that you are condemned to failure. Even when you seem to get control of this particular problem, the basic error still remains and will manifest in some other way.*

You believe that you are a body right now, but this is not the truth. You will learn the truth as you give the body the purpose of learning the truth. You are doing this now. When you asked Me to help you see this differently from the way that you have in the past, you chose a different purpose for the body. As you continue to make this new choice, I will continue to correct your thinking. The truth is that you made insane rules to govern a body that does not exist. Can you, who are the Son of God, really be governed by those rules? Only if you choose to, but absolutely, if you so choose. The only way out of this is to change your mind, and as this becomes your true desire, I will help you.

[I feel conflicted, because I really do want to maintain a certain weight, but I don't know how to feel about that. Should I not want this? I know that I am using the body to make me happy, but I also know that when I have tried not to care, I was kidding myself.]

I am not asking you to change your behavior. It is possible for you to diet and fall off your diet, to lose weight and to gain weight, and not to attach judgment to it. It is not your weight or what you eat that makes you happy or unhappy. If you judge the effect of your thoughts and find yourself wanting, you will be unhappy. If you judge the effect of your thoughts and are happy with what you see, you will be temporarily happy, and that happiness will be tempered by the certainty that is not going to last. If you do not judge the effects at all, they will not have the power to affect your happiness. It is only your thoughts that affect you.

If you want to diet, do so. Do it joyfully. Do it without guilt. Your conflict is not about whether to diet or not, it is about whether to give up control by choosing against the ego. This is a non-choice. You are deciding between your self and your Self. It is the kind of circular thinking that you are using to prop up your belief that you are a body and that you are not responsible for being a body. It is okay to be where you are, Myron, and I will always be there with you. Whatever you are doing in the illusion, keep asking Me to help you see clearly. That way, whatever purpose the ego gives it, you will be giving it another purpose, and you will be using it to awaken.

Me: Thank You for helping me. Thank You for meeting me where I am, and for letting me know that it is okay to be there. I am trying to be as patient with myself as You are.

2011

In assessing how I feel about this lesson now, as opposed to 2009, I looked at my thoughts on dieting. It took all this time to learn to see this differently. No, it wasn't about learning. It took all this time to step aside from what I believed and thought would save me, and place my trust in One Who knows. I don't know if this is complete or if I will need to look at this issue again at times, but right now I am very comfortable with where I am.

I have decided I don't know what I should weigh or why. I have thrown away the charts that would tell me and the diet aids that would help me achieve it. I have quit telling myself that there are health concerns I should be aware of, and when I read some new article expounding on another, I watch my mind to see what needs to be healed.

When I seem to be hungry, I ask, "What should I eat?" Then I follow my feelings without thinking about it. I don't seem to be guided to eat a lot of the things I used to love, like cake. If I am eating at a restaurant, which I often am, and I see Key lime pie on the menu, I feel a strong desire to eat some. So I ask again, what should I eat? Sometimes the desire is just an echo of the past.

If I am uncertain, I tell Holy Spirit that if this is not something I am being directed to eat, then help me to see it differently. And what seems to happen is that my attraction to it fades away. If I eat it anyway, I don't fall into guilt about it, and, in fact, I don't pay attention to what the mind says about it at all. Who thinks there is a law that says I should never eat Key lime pie? Who feels guilty when I do? There are no laws but God's, so this must be the ego, and I am not that.

I have changed my focus when it comes to food and to the size of my body. I have remembered that I have one purpose and that nothing is outside of that purpose, including this. My purpose is not to make laws and then follow them – or not. My purpose is not to reach a weight goal or make my body more attractive or healthier through following these laws. My only purpose is to use whatever is in front of me to awaken from the dream of separation.

I realize, from paying attention to my thoughts, that I still believe I am the body, I care what happens to it, as if the loss of the body is the loss of me. I care about other people's bodies. When my sister-in-law had a brush with death, I saw that I was fearful of losing "her" if her body died. I am still afraid of heights, so I guess I am still afraid of my own death. I still have a visceral reaction when I hear that someone is diagnosed with Alzheimer's, so I still think that I am my brain and that I could not be happy if this diagnosis were my own.

I am glad to see the proof of these beliefs so that I know what yet needs to be healed. I am willing to surrender my mistaken beliefs and to have them corrected by the Holy Spirit. I am willing to do this, even as I notice my fear to do it. Holy Spirit, I am willing to know that I am under no laws but God's. Please help my unwillingness.

Lesson 77

I am entitled to miracles.

Miracles are not about changing the world or the body. They are about changing the mind. They are about learning to choose the Holy Spirit over the ego. When I do that, my mind changes and everything is different. My unhappiness is the result of errors in thinking. To have happiness, I must allow those errors to be corrected. The result is a miracle.

I am supposed to have miracles. The Holy Spirit is in my mind, so that He can help me change those erroneous thoughts. In fact, this has already been done. We are at the end looking back. I am entitled to miracles, because they are already a done deal. My mind is changed. The miracle is in my mind waiting for me to accept it.

When I see the effects of erroneous thoughts in my life, I know that I need a miracle. I need to see differently and watch the miraculous change. The miracle is mine for the asking. Today I will ask.

Holy Spirit: Many times you have experienced the miracle of changing your mind. Sometimes it seemed hard, but it was always your resistance that caused it to be difficult. Once you stopped resisting, it simply was. That is the way it always is. The miracle simply waits for your acceptance. The more often you accept miracles, the less resistance you will have to them. Their glad results will motivate you to lower your resistance much more quickly. When you feel like you are being denied a miracle, remember that this is your own resistance. Be willing to change your mind about that, and it will be done. If you cannot yet choose joy over pain, then forgive yourself for this. Be gentle and loving to yourself. Be infinitely patient. I am.

Me: I am always astounded that I still can resist Your help, but I am becoming more patient with myself thanks to You.

A little more:

This morning my throat is sore and I am having trouble speaking. This has been going on for several weeks now. I am willing to release the belief behind this manifestation. I asked for help, and here is one thought I received. I was created unlimited, vast, without boundaries. To experience separation it was necessary for me to create boundaries. It is like I drew lines, made a box in which I see myself existing. I revise that box in every moment with each thought I accept as truth and give value to. I erase that box as I remember my true nature. The dimensions of that box are a symbol of my acceptance or rejection of myself as Spirit.

When I asked the Holy Spirit to look at the issue concerning my voice I was asking Him to look with me at a line that I have drawn, which has placed limits on the unlimited. I have done the impossible and so it is not truth, but it is my experience, because it is the experience I want. Experiencing the clearly impossible as if it were possible and real is an expression of my unlimited Self.

As I watched my thoughts, I noticed fear coming up. When I expressed a willingness to look more closely at that fear I saw that it was a fear of not speaking. I love to speak. I love to share what Spirit gives me. I love to use my voice to help others. I use my voice to earn my living. So I am afraid of losing my voice.

What I saw next was a long narrow box, which represented myself as a speaker. I am defining myself as one who fits only within that box. I am one who speaks. I am one who is a speaker. I am one who receives praise, love, acceptance, a sense of purpose, and meaning from speaking. As I realized these things, I saw in my mind's eye this box being drawn with bold dark lines, lines it would be hard to obscure or erase or even expand. I saw the box being embellished and made more attractive, even beautiful. But it still remained just a box with very firm limits.

Then I stood back from the box and saw that it existed within a brilliant light that did not seem to end. I could not find its edges. I saw that I am not that box with its boundaries so clearly defined. I am not the one who must speak to be. I am not the one who is defined by what, if anything, I say. I am not that. Rather, I am the light, unlimited and brilliant, and I have no lines that I did not draw myself. There is no box that I did not freely step into, and the box is without substance. It is just imaginary lines drawn around a small bit of the light which I am, created by a thought of a box, and easily erased by the thought of no box.

Well, that is what I have gotten so far. Once again I see that I am that I Am, and nothing else is true.

Lesson 78

Let miracles replace all grievances.

Each grievance I have stands between me and my awareness of God. My grievances are the way in which I hold on to my specialness. The day I release grievances is the day I cease to exist as an individual. It becomes clear why I am reluctant to let them go, even though they are so destructive. I tell myself that I hold on to them because they seem to be my defense against my brother's ill intentions, but really I hold on to them because they are my defense against God's love.

Each grievance is an opportunity for me to practice letting it go and to experience the miracle that stands behind it. That miracle is a change of mind, a change that will inevitably lead me to the truth that I want to return to God. I need each of these separate opportunities, so that my steps will be small and manageable. Jesus has made it clear that I will find a sudden awakening too frightening.

Since my brother is presenting me with opportunities to forgive, he is my savior. These forgiveness opportunities will return my awareness to God. In seeing my guilt mirrored in my brother, I am given the chance to forgive myself through forgiving him. Then he is given the chance to see his innocence in my forgiveness. Together we return our awareness, first to our own oneness, and then to our oneness in God. I owe my brother only my gratitude.

There is not a moment in the day that doesn't offer me an opportunity to see the miracle that stands behind the grievance. If nothing else is clear to me, I know that I hold a grievance against everyone. No one is free from my hatred. And how could it be any other way? Everyone exists as a means of displacing what I hate most about myself.

Whatever there is in me that I am too ashamed or too afraid to look at, I project onto some splintered part of my self, someone I think of as "other". I pretend that that is not me, but is outside me, and then I pretend that the guilty thing I see in them has nothing to do with me. And yet, deep, deep in my mind is the truth. How could I not hate them for being the reminder of something in me so awful that I cannot even acknowledge it?

I can strengthen the guilt that I feel by making myself wrong for my feelings. Or I can see this as the blessing it is and use every mean thought as an opportunity to forgive. I can look, with the gentle help of Jesus, at what I deny in myself and let him show me the miracle behind it. This is the healing I want.

Holy Spirit: There is no person who stands outside of forgiveness. The most awful sin you can imagine is still just a mistaken thought. I honor your desire to see the innocence of your brother, rather than the sin you imagine they committed. I stand with you, as you look at what you thought was done to you, with a willingness to see the miracle instead. I assure you that the one who you thought victimized you is really your savior, and now you are his savior.

Me: I no longer want vengeance or retribution. I only want for both of us to be saved from our self-hate and self-condemnation. I am willing to see in my brother and me only what You see, and I ask that You help me to do this.

Lesson 79

Let me recognize the problem so it can be solved.

There is only one problem – I think I separated myself from God. There is only one answer – the Holy Spirit within my mind. The Holy Spirit is the link to the truth that was placed in the mind when we entered the dream. The Holy Spirit is our memory of God's love, the only answer to the only problem. All of the millions of problems that I encounter in my life are really only one problem. I have projected the one problem onto a world that seems to be outside of me and made it look like it is many different problems and that each demands a different solution.

The purpose of doing this is to keep the problem away from the solution and to keep me distracted, so that I don't notice what I have done. If I spend my life trying to solve each seemingly outward problem with something from a world that seems to be outside my mind, then I don't have to worry about the one problem ever getting solved, because it is IN my mind, along with the solution. Why do I want to keep the problem? If I solve the problem, my life as a body and a personality is over, and I still believe I want to be an individual.

I will see every perceived problem for what it is. This morning I was thinking about how much I love taking my morning shower. I love being able to wash away the soil from yesterday, and metaphorically I wash away the problems from yesterday and start this day anew. If I could not have the shower, I would think that it was a problem. I notice that I have placed the problem outside my mind.

If my happiness depends on solving the shower problem, then I have an unsolvable problem. I cannot possibly know that a shower is going to be available to me every day. What if I am late for work and can't take one? What if there is a problem with the hot water heater? What if I never have a shower problem, but only the fear of a shower problem? No solution for that one. And this is just one of the many problems I will be presented with today.

If the problem is seen as outside my mind, and if each problem is seen as different from the one before, then I am destined to spend my life running around trying to fix problems and failing. No matter how many I fix, there is always another one, or the fear of another one. I have absolutely guaranteed that I will have a stressful, unproductive life in which I fail to accomplish anything… and then I die.

Instead, I will recognize that the shower is not the problem. The problem is not outside my mind at all. The problem is that I think I am separated from God; I have the solution right there in my mind alongside the problem. I give the Holy Spirit the thought that I have a problem with something that seems to be outside my mind and that I think I can solve the problem in the world. He gently and lovingly corrects that thought and helps me to understand that my only problem is the mistaken belief that I could be separate from God.

I give Him the thought that I want to be separated from God, that I want to be an individual with private thoughts and lots of choices, separate from all the other fragments of myself. The solution to this one problem is in my mind, and so when I stop trying to make it into a billion other problems with no solution, all existing outside my mind, I will bring it back to my mind where it is solved. All I need to do is recognize what and where the problem is. That is my only job.

Holy Spirit: Every time you experience your body as sick, you really believe you are separated from God's love. Every time you think you have been offended, you really believe you are separated from God's love. Every time you are upset because you don't have enough money, or your car has broken down, or your boss is angry with you, your problem is really that you believe you are separated from God's love.

All of the problems you have projected onto what you think of as the world are just a distraction from this one thought: you think you are separated from God's love. You are afraid of the problem, and you do not acknowledge it. You are afraid of the solution, so you very carefully keep the problem and the solution separate. This is the source of all of your unhappiness and all of your sickness.

The solution is simple: each time that you notice any discomfort within your mind, bring that thought to Me. Ask Me what the problem is, and ask Me for the solution. I want you to learn that you do not have problems in the world. That is not where they are. It is futile to spend your life trying to solve these many problems.

It is your purpose to recognize that each one represents the One problem and is not in the world at all but is in your mind, and that the solution is in your mind as well. Bringing the problem and the solution together is the answer to your problem. There is, of course, no world, and there is no endless list of seemingly insoluble problems, but since you believe that there are, the best way to use them is to bring them to Me, so that I can show you the truth.

Me: I will use the problems that pop up today for this purpose. I seem to have a grasp on this, and I want to practice it so that it stays with me. I understand that this is a very simple concept and that it is hard for me to hold on to, because I don't entirely want the solution. I give You that thought, Holy Spirit, and ask that You correct it. The real problem is that I think I am separated from God. I give You that thought, as well, Holy Spirit, and ask that You help me to know the truth.

Lesson 80

Let me recognize that my problems have been solved.

Yesterday was a practice of seeing that my problems are not out there, as I thought they were, but are in my mind, and that the solution to my problems is also in my mind. So when I thought that I had a problem in the world, I reminded myself that there is only one problem, and that is my perceived separation from God. There is only one solution, and that is the Holy Spirit within my mind, which knows there is no separation.

Today I am adding the thought that my problem has been solved. The world was over long ago, and what I think is my existence is just a memory of that world. So the problem has been solved. As I bring all the problems I perceive in the world to the truth that is in my mind, I start to remember that I have no problems, I had one problem, and it has already been solved.

While writing this, I suddenly became very aware of a sound that was disturbing me. I felt a strong irritation and stopped what I was doing to shut off the noise. As I did so, I automatically said to myself that I thought the sound was my problem, but my problem is that I think I am separated from God. Let me recognize the problem has been solved.

Even as I stopped the noise, I realized that one minute before I had not even noticed the noise, even though it had been going on since I awoke. I was using the noise to prove that Jesus was wrong. See, I do have a problem; it is noisy in here. I need to stop writing about this and do something about it. This proves that Jesus is wrong and I am right.

I am right about being an individual body with a personality, a will of its own outside God's Will, with many options from which to choose, and I can solve my problems. This may have seemed like a simple problem with a simple solution, but it was really my proof and defense against God. This is what all problems are, and the size and complexity are just camouflage against this truth.

I don't have to do anything to correct this error. I just need to accept the truth that is in my mind. Looking at it this way, choosing to keep the problem outside of myself and refusing to see the solution, makes no sense at all. I get to go on pretending that I am right. I get to go on pretending that I exist and God does not. But at what cost? I am, in effect, choosing chaos, fear, guilt, anger, depression and death. Choosing to see that the problem is not out there but in my mind, and that the problem was long ago solved, and that the solution is also in my mind waiting for me to accept, will bring me undisturbed peace, complete joy and total freedom. It is obviously a choice between sanity and madness.

Me: Holy Spirit, I am amazed that I didn't see this clearly before. It is not complicated, and it is really obvious. But what I notice is that I begin my day enthusiastically practicing the lesson, then as the day wears on, I begin to feel tired, and it starts to feel like a burden. Why is that?

Holy Spirit: Myron, you are beginning to believe this, and within you is the thought that believing the problem has been solved represents a loss for you. This is the same thought that thinks you are an ego and that there is value in being an ego. When you start to withdraw your belief from this thought, it is natural for fear to come up. Do not be disturbed about it; simply recognize that this is just another form of the one problem and that it has already been solved.

The reason you feel tired and burdened is that you are in conflict, and conflict is wearying. In a sense it is like you are in a war, but the combatants are both you. You fight yourself, as both the Holy Spirit and the ego are in your mind. It is very frustrating for the ego, because it battles with all it has, and the Holy Spirit remains at peace with no acknowledgment of the ego's fierce struggles against it. The part of you that is weary is the part that identifies with the ego. As you continue to do the lessons, you will lose that sense of connection with the thought of the ego, and the sense of struggle will go with it.

Me: I will use the problems that pop up today for this purpose. I seem to have a grasp on this, and I want to practice it so that it stays with me. I understand that this is a very simple concept and that it is hard for me to hold on to, because I don't entirely want the solution. I give You that thought, Holy Spirit, and ask that You correct it. The real problem is that I think I am separated from God. I give You that thought as well, Holy Spirit, and ask that You help me to know the truth.

Review II

Introduction

Dear God,
Up until now I have wanted freedom and yet have defended myself against it through resistance to these lessons. I have done the lessons, and I have forgotten to do the lessons. I have given them my full attention and vigilance, and I have chosen against them. My mind is split, and I have come down on Your side one moment, and on the ego side the next. But I now realize that I want to know Your Love. I may still waver, but I will not fail. I give You all the willingness I have, and I will feed that willingness by faithfully doing the lessons for the rest of the year. It is my intention to give my full attention to the review and to the rest of the lessons in this book.

Thank You, God. I love You, God.

Lesson 81

I am the light of the world. Forgiveness is my function as the light of the world.

Holy Spirit: Allow your holiness to shine forth in each thought, word and action. Let today be as holy as you are in truth. Do not allow littleness to intrude upon your kindness.

Everything you seek can be found in forgiveness. You want peace. You want to experience God. You want to feel His love and comfort. Forgiveness is the way. Don't try to define this, just give it your willingness. You recognize wrong-minded thinking; when you notice it bring it to Me for correction. This is forgiveness.

I am delighted to realize that I really get this lesson. I know that I am the light of the world, and that is my only function. I know that whatever is happening in my story, my job is to forgive it. I really know this! I might temporarily forget, just as I did before, and become upset about what appears to be happening, as was the case yesterday. I became very concerned about a threat to my job, but even in my upset, I remembered my function, and I knew that defending my job was not that function.

I spent the day returning to my practice. Each time my mind wandered to the fear about my job, I reminded myself that there is only one problem: I think I am separated from God. Then I turned to the Holy Spirit, and He would remind me that I am part of God and that this could never change. Where in God would I find fear? If fear is not in God, the fear must not be real.

No matter how many times I wandered into darkness, I forgave the situation and myself, thus I remembered my function. I used to think that because I wandered back into ego, I was failing this Course, but now I understand that my function as the light of the world is to forgive. So as long as I am forgiving when I return to fear, guilt and other forms of darkness, I am fulfilling my function.

Lesson 82

The light of the world brings peace to every mind through my forgiveness. Let me not forget my function.

It is easy to know when forgiveness is needed. Am I peaceful? Do I feel a sense of oneness with everyone and everything? If not, then I have forgiveness work to do. I have the whole world as a classroom. Any time I judge anything, I have an opportunity to practice forgiveness.

If I forget, then I know that I chose forgetfulness in order to hold on to my specialness. There is no reason to feel guilty about this. I only need to notice it with a willingness to see differently.

Jesus makes it clear that my forgetting and choosing the wrong teacher does not change my function in any way. I can ignore my function, but it remains in my mind, because the Holy Spirit remains in my mind, and what has no real effects cannot be sin and cannot be cause for guilt.

Me: Holy Spirit, do I ever get to the end of forgiveness? It seems like as soon as I forgive in one area, another pops up.

Holy Spirit: Yes, the ending is certain. It seems that you have many things to forgive, but there is only one thing masquerading as many. Don't forget that there is one problem, one solution. You believe you are separated from your Creator. That is the only thing you need forgive.

The many things you seem to be forgiving are simply the effects of the one problem. You think you are separated from your Father, and so you see guilty brothers everywhere you look. You see sickness in yourself and others. You see all forms of lack, because you do not know that you are one with God. If you knew that you were one with God, what could you possibly lack? Remember this: If what you see does not reflect God, then it cannot be real, and you cannot actually be seeing it. Forgive yourself your illusions.

Lesson 83

My only function is the one God gave me. My happiness and my function are one.

I have only one function, and fulfilling that function is what brings me happiness. This is a lesson of absolutes. Forgiveness is not "a" function; it is "the" function. There is no other function. My function is not one of the things that make me happy; it is the only thing that makes me happy.

I have chosen to distract myself with so many goals. I need to make a certain amount of money. I must do certain things to prove I am a good mom. I have a weight goal. And the great lie is that all of these goals must be met for me to be happy. This day I am willing to see that these are things I do, they are unimportant and not my goal. Doing them or not doing them is not going to affect my happiness. Only the release of guilt is going to make me happy. I accept my function of forgiveness as my only function and my only path to happiness.

There are things to be done in the world, but they are unimportant in and of themselves. The only importance they hold for me is the opportunity they present to help me awaken. Yesterday I had an unpleasant experience with the dentist. It doesn't mean anything. It did not make me happy or unhappy. My thoughts about it give the only meaning it has for me.

I chose to use it to practice letting go of my attachment to the body. I practiced using the body, rather than being the body. In this way I was forgiving the meaning I had given such things in the past, and I was fulfilling my function. Now when I think of the dentist's appointment, I don't think about the discomfort or the fear; I think about letting go and how happy that makes me. I am happy to know with a little more certainty that I am not this body. I am that I Am and not a bit less than that. What a glorious and holy hour I spent in that dental chair!

Holy Spirit: Indeed it seems that some of these things make you happy. It seems that the lack of these things makes you unhappy. It will seem this way if that is your decision, but your decision affects only your experience of it. The truth is completely unaffected by your belief, and so it is held safe for you. Happiness only awaits your glad acceptance.

Me: Holy Spirit, after the dentist had finished, I felt shaky and strange. It was a purely physical reaction, but it affected how I felt. While in the chair, I noticed each fearful thought and felt willing to see differently and willing to let go of that definition of self. I was even willing to see pain differently, and I did do that. Even with the fear and discomfort, I still felt uplifted as I stayed connected to You. Why did I have that physical reaction afterwards? Also, why did I tell people about my physical experience, rather than the only meaningful experience I had in the dental chair? I feel bad about that. Instead of sharing the miracle, I shared the lie.

Holy Spirit: When the fear came into your mind, you started to distract yourself and to try to suppress the fear. Instead, you allowed the fear to pass through you. You accepted the feeling that was triggered by the circumstances. Then you remembered to use that reaction to help you further your awakening process. You listened to My Voice when I suggested that you relax the body. Do you remember that? Where do you think such impulses come from? You were in touch with your Desire to awaken. For that I thank you. We all thank you.

The shakiness and sluggishness was simply a physical reaction to the stress that the body was under. It is nothing to be concerned about and does not mean you failed. While you were in the dental chair, you kept reminding yourself that you are not that. You are not the body, nor the experience of the body. You are not the fear of the experience. This reminder helped you to detach from the ego identification, which says that you are the body, the patient, the pain, and the fear.

When you got out of the chair, you returned to identifying with the body and the experience. You forgot that you simply participated in the body's experience, and returned to believing that you were the experience. That is why you told the story of your pain and fear; you returned to living as if you were that story. But did you notice that, even when you were telling the story, you were outside of that moment, watching yourself with an awareness of what you were doing. You chose to step into the story and be distracted by the body's responses to stress, but you did not lose sight of what was happening. You knew that this was not what you wanted to do, even while you did it.

Because of this awareness, and because you allowed yourself to see it, you will not respond in the same way the next time. Each time you are willing to look directly at your self, you leave some of that self behind, and the Self grows in your awareness. In the story you have called your life, you had an unexpected dental incident and were able to use it to help you shake off your sleep.

In Heaven we see only that you used an ordinary moment in your story to come more fully alive. In your story a lot of things happened, but in Heaven we see that only one thing happened: You remembered that you were not the body or the experience, and now you are no longer the same. You slipped momentarily back into the story, but you were not able to believe it, and you will not return to believing it, even though you will continue to experience it. This changes everything.

Lesson 84

Love created me like itself. Love holds no grievances.

I am created like God, as Love. I cannot experience this of myself if I am holding grievances. Who I am does not change, but I remain unaware of the truth until I release grievances.

Grievances can come in disguises. I was sharing with my mind-healing partner and noticed that I was becoming impatient because she just was not "getting" what I was saying. That is a grievance. I seemed to be out of peace, because she did not understand what I was saying or was not accepting it. In other words, I was saying that I was not happy and it was her fault.

I became quiet and waited for guidance before I spoke again. Later, when doing this lesson, I realized that this was a form of a grievance, and that I did not hold on to it. After asking for help, I completely let go of the need for my friend to understand or agree with me. I returned to peace.

Another part of this lesson that stands out to me is the line: "I cannot suffer, I cannot experience loss and I cannot die, I am not a body." In the past when I read things like this, I would immediately compare this statement to my life and, of course, they were not congruent. I would think of the words as affirmations or, at best, goals I was working toward.

Now I see this differently. Those words are the absolute truth. What I seem to be experiencing are the effects of the separation belief. They are the illusion. These effects are a veil drawn over the truth. They hide the truth, but do not change it. I am not the veil. I am not one who suffers and dies. I am not that. I am no longer looking at the life of Myron and thinking, "my life", and when I do, sooner or later I remember this is not true. I am detaching from the false "I" thought, and remembering the truth.

Lesson 85

My grievances hide the light of the world in me. My salvation comes from me.

This review is continuing a discussion about grievances. My grievances keep me in darkness and block the light. If I want to see, I must give up my grievances. There is a part of my mind that clings to grievances as if they were my savior, but there is a part that wants the light. As I choose to listen to Jesus, instead of to the ego, I strengthen the part of my mind that is willing to trade specialness for holiness.

Holy Spirit: There is a need to expand your thinking about grievances, because grievances are what block the light in your mind. You work with the specific grievances you see in your life, and you begin to understand that they are all the same, simply dressed up to look different. It was an ego strategy to keep you busy, so that you would be unaware of what the grievances were hiding. You know that you are starting to see the sameness. That is why you found Lessons 79 and 80 so useful; it helped you to recognize more fully the sameness of all problems.

Me: I am pretty excited about the shift that is occurring in my work with grievances. I have been handing over thought-errors for a long time now, and I have been fully convinced of the value in doing so, but when I first started, I was looking at each thought as if it were unrelated to the others. It felt like a job for hundreds of lifetimes. Thank You for helping me to see this differently.

I was reading *The Holy Spirit's Interpretation of the New Testament (NTI)* this morning, and this is what I read about Light:

> *Have faith in your Father and look to your brother for the Light. It was your Father that placed it there with him, and so it is there, within your brother where it must be.*
> *John 5*

This passage helped me to see that if I am not seeing the Light in my brother, then I must be hiding it with a grievance in my mind, because the Light is there.

Over the years during which I have been journaling these lessons, I have broadened my definition of grievances. I began by thinking of a grievance as a reaction to something someone did to me. For instance, I recognized that I was holding a grievance against my son, when I felt upset that he had not called in a long time. I then expanded it to my reaction to other situations.

An example is realizing this: I was holding a grievance against the situation that seemed to be causing my distress; I was upset that I was not being called. In both of those cases I asked the Holy Spirit to correct my thinking, and I realized it was not the person or the situation that caused my distress, but rather my thoughts about the person and situation that caused me to be upset. My mind returned to peace.

My understanding of grievances has broadened even more. I now understand that anything which blocks my awareness of Love's presence in my mind can be called a grievance. The grief I have been experiencing since my mother's death is a grievance. By not blocking or resisting the grief, by simply allowing it to flow through me without obstruction, and by remembering to ask for healing as it came into my awareness, I have begun to experience clarity about this.

The sanity in my mind does not recognize death or loss. It sees that nothing has changed, except my choice of how to see my mom now. If I insist that she is only a body and a part of my story, then I experience a sense of loss, and I grieve. This is the source of my grievance.

That insane part of my mind that does not acknowledge eternity and oneness has a grievance against my mother for leaving, and against the "something" that has taken my mother from me. It holds a grievance against "life" for being so cruel. The sane part of my mind knows that this isn't the truth, but it does not reign supreme yet.

Holy Spirit, thank You for showing me this. I want to say that I know this grievance is not the truth, and yet I grieve, so obviously there is still the thought in my mind that I can and do suffer loss. I have a grievance against life as defined by my beliefs. Please heal my mind. *Let me not use this as a block to sight.*

I am willing to give up this grievance. I have been mistaken that it has some value as a protective device. My grievance does not protect me or accord me control as I must have thought it did. I give You this mistaken thought and invite You to correct it. *I want to see.*

Lesson 86

Only God's plan for salvation will work. Holding grievances is an attack on God's plan for salvation.

I accept responsibility for my unhappiness. I make no exceptions to this. I chose to project my guilt onto others and attack them for it. This was an insane attempt to get rid of the pain. My anger and justifications for attack teach me that I am a body and that all my problems are someone else's fault and outside my mind, where I can do nothing about them.

To undo this, I return to the source of my pain, which is a thought in my mind. I tell the Holy Spirit that I am not at peace with this thought and ask that He help me see it differently. He helps me see that what upsets me in the other person is something within myself that I have split off and tried to put outside myself. Now I can ask that the Holy Spirit correct this thought.

I can apply this today by realizing that every un-peaceful thought is the result of my trying to rid my mind of guilt through projection. I can withdraw those projections and see them at their source, which is my mind, and ask for correction. I can refuse to make exceptions, no matter how tempting.

Me: Holy Spirit, I am always a little nervous about making these commitments for the day. I am afraid that I am asking for painful lessons.

Holy Spirit: I will never add to your pain. God does not ask for sacrifice. It may seem to you that this is what happens. You are learning about a thing, and suddenly the very circumstances that would help you learn appear in your life. These circumstances and ones like them have always been in your life. You are just learning to recognize them. All circumstances are opportunities to learn. Step into and through the pain and you will learn how much of an illusion it is. All pain is self-inflicted, and you are using these lessons to learn that you can make another choice.

Me: So, You seem to be saying that You are not making things happen in my life so that I can learn another way, but that I am making things happen which hurt me, and You are using these things to teach me how to not hurt myself.

Holy Spirit: Yes. That is right.

Thank You.

Lesson 87

I will there be light. There is no will but God's.

I am reminded that while I may still sometimes identify with the ego-will (wishes), I do have a will that is the Will of God. The Holy Spirit safeguards that will. I can get in touch with that will, and why not; it is my real will and it is my mind. By exercising my will, I will see everything differently. Instead of seeing people who wish me harm, I will see my brothers calling for love. I will see that we are all joined in the common purpose of returning home.

In recognizing that my real will is the same as the Will of God, I will know that I am perfectly safe, because that is His Will. When I identify with ego-wishes, I see only danger everywhere I look, because the ego knows only guilt and punishment.

As always, I need to be vigilant for guilt and fear thoughts, so that I can be aware of when I am identifying with ego. How can I even know I need to change my mind, unless I am aware of the error? I am going to remind myself that I am no longer willing to trade peace, joy and love for the specialness of being separate. I will remind myself that I still have my true will and that I want to identify with that will now.

Me: Holy Spirit, I know that when I accuse someone else of making me unhappy, I am attacking that person and choosing ego's wishes over God's Will. I know that forgiveness is called for, but I sometimes become uncertain of what is meant by that. Could You please talk to me about this?

Holy Spirit: It becomes clear, if you remember the reason you accuse someone of hurting you. You think that you need them to be guilty, instead of you. When you believe the ego's lie that you have sinned against God, you feel burdened with an unbearable sense of guilt. Your brother seems to attack you, because that is what you want him to do.

You want him to attack you, so that you can say, "Look what you did to me. See, you are the guilty one." Then you seem to have proven that guilt is not in you, but outside you. This is why you forgive your brother for what he has NOT done. You have actually done it to yourself in order to make him guilty so that you can convince yourself that the guilt is not in you, but in him.

When you feel that anyone is guilty of anything, ask yourself, "What is this for?" Why do I need my brother to be guilty? You will find that it is always for making him guilty instead of you. Forgive him for what he did not do, and allow me to help you see the truth, that you are not guilty, either.

Me: This is really clear to me for the first time. Thank You so much. But still I notice resistance to this. It is not what I want to hear. And yet when I think about specific circumstances, I see how true it is for me. For the longest time I held a grievance against my ex-husband for the direction our marriage took and for the effect it had on our children. It was very easy for me to see him as guilty because of his behavior, but as I began to practice forgiveness, I let go of my need to find him guilty. Then I began to see his behavior differently. He was simply living out his story and learning his lessons. There was nothing for me to forgive, really, other than my projections onto him.

I also realized how much I was afraid to look at my own responsibility. Then I was able to see why I thought I needed him to be guilty. I thought that as long as he was guilty there was nothing within me to look at; but in my heart I knew that I was kidding myself, so I was never truly happy. When I finally let him off the hook and looked at my own guilt, I was able to forgive completely, even myself. When I could see that he was not guilty, I was able to see that I wasn't either. Just like him, I was living my story and learning my lessons. There was really nothing to forgive.

Lesson 88

The light has come. I am under no laws but God's.

There is a strong emphasis in this review on the fact that I always seem to be choosing which reality I want to ascribe to, the ego's or God's. It also emphasizes that only God's reality truly exists. The ego's version of what is real is just an illusion and has never existed. I am spending my life believing in something that isn't there.

"I am under no laws but God's" is really saying the same thing. I made up all sorts of laws and then said that they were true and believed them and acted like they were true. Jesus says that I am free to choose differently and that He will help me do so.

It is hard to believe that the ego's version of life does not really exist, because the darkness seems so real to me. I really feel hurt when someone doesn't like me. I really think that some people are jerks and some are just plain mean. All the evidence seems to prove this. I really think that if I drink poison I will get sick and that if you sneeze on me I will catch what you have. Then I do it to prove that I am right and Jesus is wrong.

Me: Holy Spirit, I have so much resistance to the idea that I am always choosing between what exists and what doesn't exist. At first I thought that I just didn't get why Jesus kept harping on this idea, and then I asked You to help me see the importance, and now I feel the resistance.

Holy Spirit: Yes, there is great resistance, because this is the cornerstone of both the ego thought-system and My thought-system. As you stand in this place, you look in one direction and you see a life of light and blissful joy and love without end. You look in the other direction and you seem to see a shadowy world of infinite choices and drama where you can be different than everything else. You really don't want to be told that this world does not exist and that it was just a brief thought in the Christ Mind, now echoed over and over again.

You don't want to think that if you blinked your eyes the world would be gone, because it can exist only as long as you give it your full attention. When you make something up, it requires a lot of effort to maintain the illusion of reality. God, on the other hand, needs no effort at all from you. It continues to exist, whether you give It your attention or not. It continues to exist when you look away from It, and It is completely unaffected by your dreams of hell. Only God is real. You continue to choose between what is real and what is merely a dream.

Me: Holy Spirit, why does this suddenly seem so frightening to me? It never was before.

Holy Spirit: You expressed your intention to understand this, and so you are now really looking at it. Before, you glanced past it, because you did not want to know the truth. Now you are willing to see it; therefore you do see. Allow yourself to experience the fear of watching the world dissolve before your eyes. You are really watching nothing happening. Do not allow your mind to retreat into pretended ignorance again. You are safe; I am with you.

Me: Holy Spirit, I can only do this for a moment, and then I have to stop. I can't believe how scary it is to contemplate a world without my illusions. I thought that this was what I wanted, but my resistance is very strong. I feel bad that I am not willing to do this. I feel like I am letting You down.

Holy Spirit: Precious one, you cannot let me down, because I don't believe in betrayal. When your granddaughter began learning to walk, she tried and then lost courage many times, going back to the safety of crawling in order to be nearer the floor. You were not angry at her for her temporary setbacks. You never doubted her for a moment. You just celebrated and encouraged her every small success. I, too, celebrate you. You showed great courage in your willingness to see. Now that you have come this far, you will never be willing to retreat into deep sleep again. You have so much help and support. The angels surround and uphold you. Heaven Itself rejoices with you.

Me: The part of my mind that still identifies with the ego is trying to pull me back into the comfort of the illusion with which

I am most familiar. It offers me specialness and someone to blame for what goes wrong. I don't want it and at first feel fear that I am going to lose the awareness I have gained this morning. I remind myself that it is just the ego and that the ego doesn't even exist. I can hear the ego voice, but I don't have to believe it or even pay attention to it. If I feel guilty for being aware of the ego-thoughts, then I will be saying that it is real and has real power. Thank You for the many insights this morning. I am so happy that it brings tears to my eyes.

2011

The light really has come. There are still shadows within my world where I retreat into darkness from time to time during the day, and occasionally for a few days. But now I never feel that I am alone in the dark. I sit in the dark a while, pretending that I don't understand my confusion, pretending that I don't know my way out, but all the time I am talking to the Holy Spirit.

How lost could I be if I know that this is not real and that the Holy Spirit is my ticket out? What He always leads me to is my true desire, the desire of my heart. As soon as I remember that the only thing worth having, the only thing I want, is to know God, whatever I need to think or do or say comes into my mind. It is only my own choice to be in hell that holds me there.

I am under no laws but God's. I also know that Myron's life will not reflect this until it is a Heart belief. As long as this statement is in the head only, I remain under my self-imposed laws. As long as this is true, I will act sensibly. I will eat healthily, take medicine when I need it, look both ways before I cross the street. If I believe I am a body or even that I am in this body, then I also believe in the laws I made to govern the body.

All the while, I notice the wrong-minded thinking that got me here and ask for healing. I practice detachment through constantly reminding myself that I am not the body, through reminding myself that I am not the ego-thoughts in my mind, and through surrender as complete as I can make it. I am slowly, but very surely, letting go of the ego-identity.

I am learning that I don't live in this world, not even in this body. I am not experiencing the life of Myron, but rather observing this life. When I know this is true and I no longer identify with the panic, the fear, the guilt and rage that is the natural effect of living under the delusion of separation, then I will KNOW that I am under no laws but God's.

Lesson 89

I am entitled to miracles. Let miracles replace all grievances.

I am not entitled to punishment, but to miracles. I can experience miracles by watching my attack thoughts with a willingness to have them corrected. As I learn that I do not want to have separate interests, but to join with my brother in the common purpose of awakening, I open my mind to the miracle of God's Love. I am choosing to see that I am wrong and God is right and that I am glad to have been wrong.

It can be really hard to accept that I don't need to be right. I see this all the time. In a discussion about a paragraph in the text, one of the group sees it differently than I do. I have to force myself to shut up. The ego's thought is "but that's not right," and the ego thought-system says that it is imperative that I be right. I've had to bite my tongue so often that it is a wonder that it is still intact. But I remind myself that I don't know what anything is for and that it is not my purpose to be right, only to join with my brother. Making him understand that he is wrong and I am right is definitely not joining in purpose. After I give this need to be right to the Holy Spirit, I suddenly can't remember why I thought that I needed to be right. Until the next time! Ha!

Holy Spirit: Separation, by definition, demands that the other person be different than you. That they are wrong and you are right further defines you as a separate and special person. Competition is a necessary component of separation, and as long as you still believe you are a body, you will experience these competitive thoughts, and believe that the outcome matters. As you choose to bring them to the light for healing, they have less effect on you, and your belief in them weakens, as does your belief in separation. You are doing exactly the right thing by noticing them, and asking for correction. The ego created competition to keep you separate, but with your decision against this, you allow the Holy Spirit to use the ego's creation to help you wake up.

Lesson 90

Let me recognize the problem so it can be solved. Let me recognize that my problems have been solved.

I am reminded that the problem and the answer are both in my mind, which is outside time and space. This lesson tells me that I do not have to wait for salvation. I imagine them in my mind, the problem superimposed over the answer, like one transparency over another. To see through a transparency to what is on the one under it just takes a shift in my vision. And so I learn to see through the problem to the answer. This visual helps me see how the solution is immediate.

This process of working with the Holy Spirit every morning is causing a shift in my thinking, and the ego is frightened by it. I am experiencing myself as tired because I am in conflict. The part of my mind that wants to wake up is excited about the shift. The part of my mind that is afraid to wake up wants me to stop before this process is irreversible. Bad news for the ego: I have already reached that point.

Me: Holy Spirit, I see that I don't have to go through any kind of formal process to receive Your words. You spoke to me very clearly without this introduction this morning. I recognized You in thoughts I was having.

Holy Spirit: Yes, that is true. I speak to you always, without ceasing. You heard Me because you did truly want to hear Me. You recognized the Source of your thoughts because you have formed the habit of listening to Me. You thought the problem was that you were tired, but the problem was that you felt separated from God. You have made it a habit to turn to Me, and so that is what you did, even though you did not say the words. The solution to your problem is right there with the problem, and so the problem was solved instantaneously. It took you a little while to accept the answer, but you chose it much more quickly than you once would have.

You were wondering about how all problems are really attacks, and this is an example of how that is. You see your resistance to God as an attack on Him. You project the guilt you feel onto your body, and now you have attacked your body. It feels tired, your sleep is disturbed, and your head hurts. The problem occurred in your mind with the mistaken thought that you could ever attack your Creator and that He holds this against you. The solution is also in your mind and says that the separation never occurred and that God loves you.

Me: I am amazed at how desperately I cling to my discomfort. Obviously, I believe that my attack is protecting me. This is so clearly insane that I don't know how I can still believe in it. I also find it very interesting to see how I have changed over the past two years. I accept You into my mind with little resistance most of the time, Holy Spirit. It feels very natural now to talk to You all through the day, and when I do not listen to You during the day, I notice that, too. I also find it easy to distinguish when I am listening to Spirit and when I am listening to ego. This morning I am filled with gratitude as I realize that, while I still experience many forms of the one problem, I am also aware of the one solution, and I am far quicker to ask for it. I am, as a result, far more peaceful and much happier.

My Final Message from Holy Spirit for this Volume

Holy Spirit: You have done well, dear one, as you have willingly stepped back and allowed Me to guide you. Continue to be patient and not strive for what you cannot fully comprehend as yet. That will avail you only confusion. The end is certain and so you can afford to be patient. And be of good cheer, as I am leading you into the experience of your true power.

Me: Thank you. I am doing my best to relinquish my sense of control, knowing that it is a false sense anyway. I give You my mind and invite You to be my Guide.